1000 THINGS YOU SHOULD KNOW ABOUT

DINOSAURS

1000 THINGS YOU SHOULD KNOW ABOUT

DINOSAURS

Steve Parker
Consultant: Dr Jim Flegg

Miles Kelly
PUBLISHING

First published in 2002 by
Miles Kelly Publishing Ltd
Bardfield Centre, Great Bardfield, Essex, CM7 4SL

Copyright © Miles Kelly Publishing 2002

2 4 6 8 10 9 7 5 3

Editorial Director: Anne Marshall
Project Manager: Ruth Boardman
Production: Estela Godoy
Picture Research: Liberty Newton
Designed and Edited by: Starry Dog Books

British Library Cataloguing-in-Publication Data
A catalogue record for this book is available from the British Library

ISBN 1-84236-089-2

Printed in China

CONTENTS

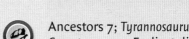
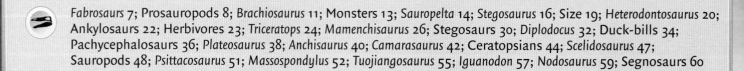
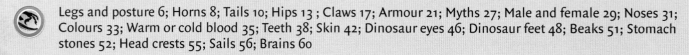
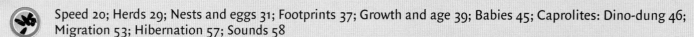
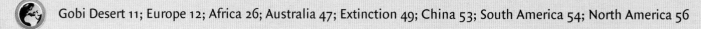
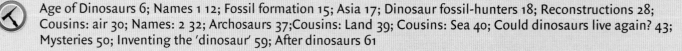

KEY

 Meat-eating dinosaurs

 Herbivorous dinosaurs

 Dinosaurs' anatomy

 Lifestyle and behaviour

 Where they lived

 Fossil finds

Age of Dinosaurs

- **The Age of Dinosaurs** corresponds to the time period that geologists call the Mesozoic Era, from about 248–65 million years ago.

- **The Mesozoic Era** is divided into three shorter time spans – the Triassic, Jurassic and Cretaceous Periods.

- **In the Triassic Period**, 248–208 million years ago, the dinosaurs began to evolve.

- **During the Jurassic Period** – about 208–144 million years ago – the dinosaurs reached their greatest size.

- **The Cretaceous Period** is when dinosaurs were at their most varied – about 144–065 million years ago.

- **In the Triassic Period**, all the continents were joined in one supercontinent – Pangaea.

- **In the Jurassic Period**, the supercontinent of Pangaea separated into two huge land-masses – Laurasia in the north and Gondwana in the south.

- **In the Cretaceous Period**, Laurasia and Gondwana split, and the continents as we know them began to form.

- **In the Mesozoic Era**, the major land-masses gradually moved across the globe in a process known as 'continental drift'.

MYA	ERA	PERIOD	
80			
100		CRETACEOUS	
120			
140	MESOZOIC	136 MYA	AGE OF REPTILES
160		JURASSIC	
180			
200		193 MYA	
220		TRIASSIC 225 MYA	

▲ *Dinosaurs ruled the land for 160 million years – longer than any other animal group.*

- **The joining and separating** of the continents affected which kinds of dinosaurs lived where.

Legs and posture

- **All dinosaurs had 4 limbs.** Unlike certain other reptiles, such as snakes and slow-worms, they did not lose their limbs through evolution.

- **Some dinosaurs**, such as massive, plant-eating sauropods like *Janenschia*, stood and walked on all four legs nearly all the time.

- **The all-fours method** of standing and walking is called 'quadrupedal'.

- **Some dinosaurs**, such as nimble, meat-eating dromaeosaurs like *Deinonychus*, stood and walked on their back limbs only. The front two limbs were used as arms.

- **The back-limbs-only method** of standing and walking is called 'bipedal'.

- **Some dinosaurs**, such as hadrosaurs like *Edmontosaurus*, could move on all four limbs or just on their back legs if they chose to.

- **The two-or-four-legs method** of standing and walking is called 'bipedal/quadrupedal'.

- **Reptiles** such as lizards and crocodiles have a sprawling posture, in which the upper legs join the body at the sides.

- **Dinosaurs** had an upright posture, with the legs directly below the body.

- **The more efficient upright posture** and gait may be one major reason why dinosaurs were so successful compared to other animals of the time.

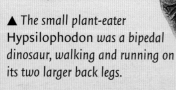

▲ *The small plant-eater Hypsilophodon was a bipedal dinosaur, walking and running on its two larger back legs.*

Fabrosaurs

- **Fabrosaurs** were small dinosaurs that lived towards the beginning of the Jurassic Period, about 208–200 million years ago.

- **The group was named** from *Fabrosaurus*, a dinosaur that was itself named in 1964, from just the fossil of a piece of lower jaw bone, found in southern Africa.

- **Lesothosaurus** was a fabrosaur, the fossils of which were found in the Lesotho region of Africa, near the *Fabrosaurus* fossil. It was named in 1978.

- **The lightly built** *Lesothosaurus* was only 1 m long from nose to tail-tip, and would have stood knee-high to an adult human.

- **Lesothosaurus** had long, slim back legs and long toes, indicating that it was a fast runner.

- **The teeth and other fossils** of *Lesothosaurus* show that it probably ate low-growing plants such as ferns.

- **Lesothosaurus's teeth** were set inwards slightly from the sides of its skull, suggesting it had fleshy cheek pouches for storing or chewing food.

- **Lesothosaurus** may have crouched down to rest on its smaller front arms when feeding on the ground.

- **Lesothosaurus** probably lived in herds, grazing and browsing, and then racing away at speed from danger.

- **Some experts believe** that *Lesothosaurus* and *Fabrosaurus* were the same, and that the two sets of fossils were given different names.

◄ *Lesothosaurus's head and neck were small in relation to its body.*

Ancestors

- **Experts have many opinions** as to which group (or groups) of reptiles were the ancestors of the dinosaurs.

- **The earliest dinosaurs** appeared in the Middle Triassic Period, about 230–225 million years ago, so their ancestors must have been around before this.

- **Very early dinosaurs** walked and ran on their strong back limbs, so their ancestors were probably similar.

★ STAR FACT ★
Creatures similar to *Euparkeria* or *Lagosuchus* may have given rise to the first dinosaurs.

- **The thecodonts** or 'socket-toothed' group of reptiles may have been the ancestors of the dinosaurs.

- **A thecodont's teeth** grew from roots fixed into pit-like sockets in the jaw bone, as in dinosaurs.

- **Some thecodonts** resembled sturdy lizards. Others evolved into true crocodiles (still around today).

- **The ornithosuchian thecodonts** became small, upright creatures with long back legs and long tails.

- **The smaller thecodonts** included *Euparkeria*, at about 60 cm long, and *Lagosuchus*, at about 30 cm long.

- **Euparkeria and Lagosuchus** were fast-moving creatures that used their sharp claws and teeth to catch insects.

◄ *The early reptile Dimetrodon was a pelycosaur, not a dinosaur.*

Prosauropods

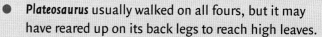

- **The prosauropods** were the first really big dinosaurs to appear on Earth. They were plant-eaters that thrived about 230–180 million years ago.

- **Prosauropods** had small heads, long necks and tails, wide bodies and four sturdy limbs.

- **One of the first prosauropods** was *Plateosaurus*, which lived about 220 million years ago in present-day France, Germany, Switzerland and other parts of Europe.

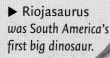

▶ Riojasaurus
was South America's first big dinosaur.

- *Plateosaurus* usually walked on all fours, but it may have reared up on its back legs to reach high leaves.

- *Plateosaurus* was up to 8 m in total length, and weighed about 1 tonne.

- **Another prosauropod** was *Riojasaurus*. Its fossils are 218 million years old, and come from Argentina.

- *Riojasaurus* was 10 m long and weighed about 2 tonnes.

- *Anchisaurus* was one of the smallest prosauropods, at only 2.5 m long and about 30 kg. It lived in eastern North America about 190 million years ago.

- **Fossil evidence** suggests that 5-m long *Massospondylus* lived in southern Africa and perhaps North America.

- **The sauropods** followed the prosauropods and were even bigger, but had the same basic body shape, with long necks and tails.

Horns

- **A dinosaur's horns** got bigger as the animal grew – they were not shed and replaced each year like the antlers of today's deer.

- **Each horn** had a bony core and an outer covering of horny substance formed mainly from keratin.

- **Horns** were most common among the plant-eating dinosaurs. They were probably used for self-defence and to defend offspring against predators.

- **The biggest horns** belonged to the ceratopsians or 'horn-faces', such as *Triceratops*.

> ★ STAR FACT ★
> Dinosaurs may have used their horns to push over plants or dig up roots for food.

- **In some ceratopsians**, just the bony core of the horn was about 1 m long, not including the outer sheath.

- **The ceratopsian** *Styracosaurus* or 'spiked reptile' had a series of long horns around the top of its neck frill, and a very long horn on its nose.

- **Horns may have been used** in head-swinging displays to intimidate rivals and make physical fighting less likely.

- **In battle**, male dinosaurs may have locked horns in a trial of strength, as antelopes do today.

- **Armoured dinosaurs** such as the nodosaur *Panoplosaurus* had horn-like spikes along the sides of its body.

◀ *Styracosaurus's frill horns had bony centres.*

Tyrannosaurus

- **Tyrannosaurus** is not only one of the most famous of the dinosaurs, but also one about which a great deal is known. Several discoveries have revealed fossilized bones, teeth, whole skeletons and other remains.

- **Tyrannosaurus** lived at the very end of the Age of Dinosaurs, about 68–65 million years ago.

- **The full name** of *Tyrannosaurus* is *Tyrannosaurus rex*, which means 'king of the tyrant reptiles'.

- **The head** of *Tyrannosaurus* was 1.2 m long and had more than 50 dagger-like teeth, some longer than 15 cm.

- **Tyrannosaurus** fossils have been found at many sites in North America, including Alberta and Saskatchewan in Canada, and Colorado, Wyoming, Montana and New Mexico in the USA.

> ★ STAR FACT ★
> *Tyrannosaurus*, when fully grown, was about 12–13 m long and stood taller than a two-decker bus. It weighed 6–7 tonnes.

- **The arms and hands** of *Tyrannosaurus* were so small that they could not pass food to its mouth, and may have had no use at all.

- **Recent fossil finds** of a group of *Tyrannosaurus*, includes youngsters, suggesting that they may have lived as families in small herds.

- **Tyrannosaurus** may have been an active hunter, pounding along at speed after its fleeing prey, or it may have been a skulking scavenger that ambushed old and sickly victims.

- **Until the 1990s,** *Tyrannosaurus* was known as the biggest meat-eating dinosaur, and the biggest meat-eating animal ever to walk the Earth, but its size record has been broken by *Giganotosaurus*.

▲ The huge skull of Tyrannosaurus *was deep from top to bottom, but relatively narrow from side to side. The jaw hinged at the rear of the head, giving a vast gape when the mouth was open.*

Curved neck allowed head to face forwards

Two-fingered 'hand'

Thick, heavy, muscular base to tail

Deep chest probably gave great stamina

Three-toed foot

▶ Tyrannosaurus's massive, *powerful rear legs contrasted greatly with its puny front limbs or 'arms'. As it pounded along, its thick-based tail balanced its horizontal body and the head, which was held low. The rear feet were enormous, each set of three toes supporting some 3–4 tonnes.*

Raptors

- **'Raptors'** is a nickname for the dromaeosaur group.

- **'Raptor'** is variously said to mean 'plunderer', 'thief' or 'hunter' (birds of prey are also called raptors).

- **Dromaeosaurs** were medium-sized, powerful, agile, meat-eating dinosaurs that lived mainly about 110–65 million years ago.

- **Most dromaeosaurs** were 1.5–3 m from nose to tail, weighed 20–60 kg, and stood 1–2 m tall.

- *Velociraptor* lived 75–70 million years ago, in what is now the barren scrub and desert of Mongolia in Central Asia.

- **Like other raptors**, *Velociraptor* probably ran fast and could leap great distances on its powerful back legs.

- **The dromaeosaurs** are named after the 1.8-m long *Dromaeosaurus* from North America – one of the least known of the group, from very few fossil finds.

- **The best-known raptor** is probably *Deinonychus*.

- **The large mouths of dromaeosaurs** opened wide and were equipped with many small, sharp, curved teeth.

> ★ STAR FACT ★
> On each foot, a dromaeosaur had a large, curved claw that it could swing in an arc to slash through its victim's flesh.

◄ *Velociraptor, the 'speedy thief', was a typical dromaeosaur. Fossils of it were found in Central Asia.*

Tails

- **All dinosaurs** evolved with tails – though some individuals may have lost theirs in attacks or accidents!

- **The length of the tail** relative to the body, and its shape, thickness and special features, give many clues as to how the dinosaur used it.

- **The longest tails**, at more than 17 m, belonged to the giant plant-eating sauropods such as *Diplodocus*.

- **Some sauropods** had a linked chain of more than

80 separate bones inside the tail – more than twice the usual number.

- **A sauropod** may have used its tail as a whip to flick at enemies.

- **Many meat-eating dinosaurs** that stood and ran on their back legs had thick-based tails to counterbalance the weight of their bodies and heads.

- **Small, fast, agile meat-eaters**, such as *Compsognathus*, used their tails for balance when leaping and darting about.

- **The meat-eater** *Ornitholestes* had a tail that was more than half of its 2-m length, and was used as a counterbalance-rudder to help it turn corners at speed.

- **The armoured dinosaurs** known as ankylosaurs had two huge lumps of bone at the ends of their tails, which they swung at their enemies like a club.

- **The tails of the duck-billed dinosaurs** (hadrosaurs) may have been swished from side to side in the water as an aid to swimming.

▶ *Compsognathus may have used its tapering, whiplike tail to slap its enemies.*

Gobi Desert

- **The Gobi** covers much of southern Mongolia and parts of northern China. During the Age of Dinosaurs, it was a land of scrub and scattered trees.

▲ The Gobi's fossil sites are far from any towns.

- **The first fossil-hunting expeditions** to the Gobi Desert took place in 1922–25, organized by the American Museum of Natural History.
- **The 1922–25 Gobi expeditions** set out to look for fossils of very early humans, but instead found some amazing dinosaur remains.
- **The first fossil dinosaur eggs** were found by the 1922–25 expeditions.
- *Velociraptor, Avimimus* and *Pinacosaurus* were discovered in the Gobi.
- **Russian fossil-hunting trips** into the Gobi Desert in 1946 and 1948–49 discovered new types of armoured dinosaurs, duck-billed dinosaurs, and the huge meat-eater *Tarbosaurus*.
- **More expeditions** to the Gobi in the 1960s–70s, especially to the fossil-rich area of the Nemegt Basin, found the giant sauropod *Opisthocoelicaudia* and the helmet headed *Prenocephale*.
- **Other dinosaurs** found in the Gobi include the ostrich-dinosaur *Gallimimus* and the strong-beaked 'egg thief' *Oviraptor*.
- **The inhospitable Gobi** can be -40°C in winter and 40°C in summer.
- **Despite the harsh conditions**, the Gobi Desert is one of the most exciting areas in the world for finding dinosaur fossils.

Brachiosaurus

- **Relatively complete** fossil remains exist of *Brachiosaurus*.
- *Brachiosaurus* was a sauropod – a huge plant-eater.
- **At 25-m long** from nose to tail, *Brachiosaurus* was one of the biggest of all dinosaurs.
- **Fossils** of *Brachiosaurus* have been found in North America, east and north Africa, and also possibly southern Europe.
- **Estimates of the weight** of *Brachiosaurus* range from about 30 to 75 tonnes.
- *Brachiosaurus* lived about 150 million years ago, and may have survived until 115 million years ago.

- **The name** *Brachiosaurus* means 'arm reptile' – it was so-named because of its massive front legs.
- **With its huge front legs and long neck**, *Brachiosaurus* could reach food more than 13 m from the ground.
- **The teeth** of *Brachiosaurus* were small and chisel-shaped for snipping leaves from trees.
- *Brachiosaurus's* nostrils were high on its head.

◀ *Brachiosaurus had similar body proportions to a giraffe, but was more than twice as tall and 50 times heavier.*

Europe

- **The first dinosaur fossils** ever discovered and given official names were found in England.

- **One of the first almost complete dinosaur skeletons** found was that

▲ The dots indicate dinosaur fossils found in Europe.

of the big plant-eater *Iguanodon*, in 1871, in southern England.

- **Some of the most numerous early fossils found** were those of *Iguanodon*, discovered in a coal mine in the Belgian village of Bernissart in 1878.

- **About 155–150 million years ago**, Solnhofen in southern Germany was a mosaic of lush islands and shallow lagoons – ideal for many kinds of life.

- **In sandstone** in the Solnhofen region of Germany, fossils of amazing detail preserved the tiny *Compsognathus* and the first known bird, *Archaeopteryx*.

- **Fossils** of tiny *Compsognathus* were found near Nice in southern France.

- **Many fossils** of the plant-eating prosauropod *Plateosaurus* were recovered from Trossingen, Germany, in 1911–12, 1921–23 and 1932.

- **Some of the largest fossil dinosaur eggs**, measuring 30 cm long (5 times longer than a hen's egg), were thought to have been laid by the sauropod *Hypselosaurus* near Aix-en-Provence in southern France.

- **The Isle of Wight** off southern England has provided so many dinosaur fossils that it is sometimes known as 'Dinosaur Island'.

- **Fossils** of *Hypsilophodon* have been found in eastern Spain, and those of *Camptosaurus* on the coast of Portugal.

Names: 1

- **Every dinosaur has a scientific name,** usually made up from Latin or Greek, and written in *italics*.

- **Many dinosaur names** end in *-saurus*, which some say means 'reptile' and others say means 'lizard' – even though dinosaurs were not lizards.

- **Dinosaur names** often refer to a feature that no other dinosaur had. *Baryonyx*, for example, means 'heavy claw', from the massive claw on its thumb.

- **The medium-sized meat-eater** *Herrerasaurus* from Argentina was named after Victorino Herrera, the farmer who first noticed its fossils.

- **Many dinosaur names are real**

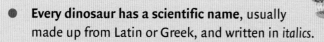

▲ *Herrerasaurus was named after the Andean farmer who found it.*

tongue-twisters, such as *Opisthocoelicaudia*, pronounced 'owe-pis-thowe-see-lee-cord-ee-ah'.

- *Opisthocoelicaudia* means 'posterior tail cavity', and refers to the joints between the backbones in the tail.

- **Some dinosaurs** were named after the place where their fossils were found. *Minmi* was located near Minmi Crossing in Queensland, Australia.

- **Some dinosaur groups** are named after the first-discovered or major one of its kind, such as the tyrannosaurs or stegosaurs.

- **The fast-running ostrich-dinosaurs'** name, ornithomimosaurs, means 'bird-mimic reptiles'.

> ★ STAR FACT ★
> *Triceratops*, or 'three-horned face', is one of the best known dinosaur scientific names.

Monsters

- **Dinosaurs** can be measured by length and height, but 'biggest' usually means heaviest or bulkiest.

- **Dinosaurs were not the biggest-ever living things** on Earth – some trees are more than 100 times their size.

- **The sauropod dinosaurs** of the Late Jurassic were the biggest animals to walk on Earth, as far as we know.

- **Sauropod dinosaurs** may not have been the biggest animals ever. Today's great whales, and perhaps the massive, flippered sea reptiles called pliosaurs of the Dinosaur Age, rival them in size.

- **For any dinosaur,** enough fossils must be found for a panel of scientists to be sure it is a distinct type, so they can give it a scientific name. They must also be able to estimate its size. With some giant dinosaurs, not enough fossils have been found.

- **Supersaurus** remains found in Colorado, USA, suggest a dinosaur similar to *Diplodocus*, but perhaps even longer, at 35 m.

- **Seismosaurus** fossils found in 1991 in the USA may belong to a 40-m long sauropod.

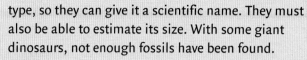

Long neck for reaching high leaves

- **Ultrasaurus** fossils found in South Korea suggest a dinosaur similar to *Brachiosaurus*, but smaller.

- **Ultrasaurus** fossils from the USA suggest a dinosaur similar to *Brachiosaurus*, but possibly even bigger.

- **Argentinosaurus** from South America may have weighed 100 tonnes or more.

▲ Seismosaurus *is known from few fossils.*

Hips

- **All dinosaurs are classified** in one of two large groups, according to the design and shape of their hip bones.

- **One of the two large groups of dinosaurs** is the Saurischia, meaning 'reptile-hipped'.

- **In a saurischian dinosaur,** the lower front pair of rod-shaped bones in the pelvis project down and forwards.

- **All meat-eating dinosaurs** belonged to the Saurischia.

- **The biggest dinosaurs,** the plant-eating sauropods, belonged to the Saurischia.

◄ *Saurischian ('reptile-hipped') bones.*

► *Ornithischian ('bird-hipped') bones.*

- **The second of the two groups of dinosaurs** is the Ornithischia, meaning 'bird-hipped'.

★ **STAR FACT** ★
One way experts assign a dinosaur to a main group is by the structure of its hip bones.

- **In an ornithischian dinosaur,** the lower front pair of rod-shaped bones in the pelvis, called the pubis bones, project down and backwards, lying parallel with another pair, the ischium bones.

- **All dinosaurs** in the group Ornithischia, from small *Heterodontosaurus* to huge *Triceratops*, were plant-eaters.

- **In addition to hips,** there are other differences between the Saurischia and Ornithischia, such as an 'extra' bone called the predentary at the front tip of the lower jaw in ornithischians.

Ostrich-dinosaurs

- **'Ostrich-dinosaurs'** is the common name of the ornithomimosaurs, because of their resemblance to today's largest bird – the flightless ostrich.

- **Ostrich-dinosaurs** were tall and slim, with two long, powerful back legs for very fast running.

- **The front limbs** of ostrich-dinosaurs were like strong arms, with grasping fingers tipped by sharp claws.

- **The eyes** of ostrich-dinosaurs were large and set high on the head.

- **The toothless mouth** of an ostrich-dinosaur was similar to the long, slim beak of a bird.

- **Ostrich-dinosaurs** lived towards the end of the Cretaceous Period, about 100–65

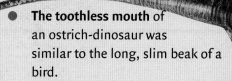

million years ago, in North America and Asia.

- **Fossils** of the ostrich-dinosaur *Struthiomimus* from Alberta, Canada, suggest it was almost 4 m in total length and stood about 2 m tall – the same height as a modern ostrich.

- **The ostrich-dinosaur** *Gallimimus* was almost 6 m long and stood nearly 3 m high.

- **Ostrich-dinosaurs probably ate** seeds, fruits and other plant material, as well as small animals such as worms and lizards, which they may have grasped with their powerful clawed hands.

- **Other ostrich-dinosaurs** included *Dromiceiomimus*, at 3–4 m long, and the slightly bigger *Ornithomimus*.

◀ Ostrich-dinosaurs such as Dromiceiomimus *were probably the fastest runners of their time, speeding along at 60–70 km/h.*

Sauropelta

- **Sauropelta** was a nodosaur – a type of armoured dinosaur.

- **The name** *Sauropelta* means 'shielded reptile', from the many large, conelike lumps of bone – some almost as big as dinner plates – on its head, neck, back and tail.

- **The larger lumps of bone** on *Sauropelta* were interspersed with smaller, fist-sized bony studs.

- **Sauropelta** had a row of sharp spikes along each side of its body, from just behind the eyes to the tail. The spikes decreased in size towards the tail.

- **Sauropelta** was about 7.5 m long, including the tail, and its

★ STAR FACT ★
Sauropelta lived 110–100 million years ago, in present-day Montana and Wyoming, USA.

bulky body and heavy, bony armour meant it probably weighed almost 3 tonnes.

- **The armour** of *Sauropelta* was flexible, almost like lumps of metal set into thick leather, so the dinosaur could twist and turn, but was unable to run fast.

- **Strong, sturdy, pillarlike legs** supported *Sauropelta*'s great weight.

- **Sauropelta** probably defended itself by crouching down to protect its softer belly, or swinging its head to jab at an enemy with its long neck spines.

- **Using its beaklike mouth,** *Sauropelta* probably plucked its low-growing plant food.

▲ Sauropelta *was heavily armoured and protected on its upper side, but not on its belly.*

Fossil formation

- **Most of the information** we know, or guess, about dinosaurs comes from fossils.

- **Fossils are the remains of once-living things** that have been preserved in rocks and turned to stone, usually over millions of years.

- **Not just dinosaurs**, but many kinds of living things from prehistoric times have left fossils, including mammals, birds, lizards, fish, insects and plants such as ferns and trees.

- **The flesh, guts and other soft parts** of a dead dinosaur's body were probably eaten by scavengers, or rotted away, and so rarely formed fossils.

- **Fossils usually formed** when a dinosaur's remains were quickly covered by sediments such as sand, silt or mud, especially along the banks of a river or lake, or on the seashore.

- **The sand or other sediment** around a creature

★ STAR FACT ★
The hard parts of a dinosaur's body were the most likely parts to form fossils, especially teeth, bones, claws and horns.

or plant's remains was gradually buried deeper by more sediment, squeezed under pressure, and cemented together into a solid mass of rock.

- **As the sediment turned to rock**, so did the plant or animal remains encased within it.

- **Information about dinosaurs** comes not only from fossils, but also from 'trace' fossils. These were not actual parts of their bodies, but other items or signs of their presence.

- **Trace fossils** include egg shells, footprints, marks made by claws and teeth, and coprolites – fossilized dinosaur droppings.

▶ Fossil formation is a very long process, and extremely prone to chance and luck. Only a tiny fraction of animals that ever lived have left remains preserved by this process. Because of the way fossils are formed, animals that died in water or along banks and shores were most likely to become fossilized. It is very rare to find all the parts of an animal arranged as they were in life. Much more often, parts have been separated, jumbled, broken, crushed and distorted.

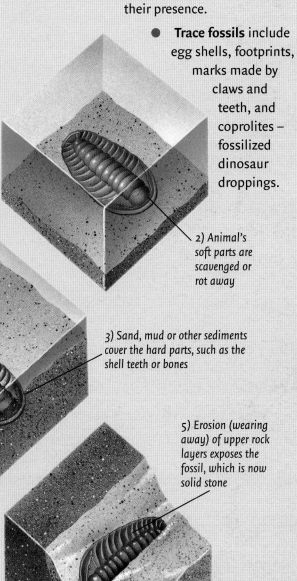

1) Animal dies and is covered by water

2) Animal's soft parts are scavenged or rot away

3) Sand, mud or other sediments cover the hard parts, such as the shell teeth or bones

4) More layers build up as the minerals in the shell and other hard parts turn to rock

5) Erosion (wearing away) of upper rock layers exposes the fossil, which is now solid stone

Stegosaurus

- ***Stegosaurus*** was the largest of the stegosaurs group.

- **Fossils** of *Stegosaurus* were found mainly in present-day Colorado, Utah and Wyoming, USA.

- ***Stegosaurus***, like most of its group, lived towards the end of the Jurassic Period, about 150 million years ago.

- **The mighty** *Stegosaurus* was about 8–9 m long from nose to tail-tip and probably weighed more than 2 tonnes.

- **The most striking feature** of *Stegosaurus* were the large roughly triangular bony plates along its back.

- **The name** *Stegosaurus* means 'roof reptile'. It was given this name because it was first thought that its 80-cm long bony plates lay flat on its back, overlapping slightly like the tiles on a roof.

- **It is now thought** that the back plates of *Stegosaurus* stood upright in two long rows.

- **The back plates** of *Stegosaurus* may have been for body temperature control, allowing the dinosaur to warm up quickly if it stood side-on to the sun's rays.

- ***Stegosaurus's*** back plates may have been covered with brightly coloured skin, possibly to intimidate enemies – they were too flimsy for protection.

- ***Stegosaurus's*** tail was armed with 4 large spikes, probably for swinging at enemies in self defence.

▶ Stegosaurus's *shorter front limbs meant that it ate low-growing plants.*

Great meat-eaters

- **The large meat-eating dinosaurs** belonged to a general group known as the 'carnosaurs'.

- **All carnosaurs** were similar in body shape, and resembled the fearsome *Tyrannosaurus*.

- ***Tarbosaurus*** was very similar to *Tyrannosaurus*. It lived at the same time, 70–65 million years ago, but in Asia rather than North America.

- **Some experts believe** that *Tarbosaurus* was an Asian version of the North American *Tyrannosaurus*, and both should have been called *Tyrannosaurus*.

- **The carnosaur** *Albertosaurus* was about 8–9 m long and lived 75–70 million years

◀ Albertosaurus *had bony ridges on its eyebrows.*

★ STAR FACT ★
Giganotosaurus lived about 100 million years ago in today's Argentina, South America.

ago, in present-day Alberta, Canada.

- ***Spinosaurus*** was a huge carnosaur from North Africa, measuring 12 m long and weighing 4–5 tonnes. It had tall, rodlike bones on its back, which may have been covered with skin, like a 'sail'.

- ***Daspletosaurus*** was a 9-m long carnosaur that lived at the end of the Age of Dinosaurs in Alberta, Canada.

- **Biggest of all the carnosaurs** was *Giganotosaurus*, the largest meat-eater ever to walk the Earth.

- ***Giganotosaurus*** was up to 16 m long and weighed at least 8 tonnes.

◀ The Asian Tarbosaurus *was almost identical to Tyrannosaurus.*

Claws

- **Like reptiles today,** dinosaurs had claws or similar hard structures at the ends of their digits (fingers and toes).

- **Dinosaur claws** were probably made from keratin – the same hard substance that formed their horns, and from which our own fingernails and toenails are made.

- **Claw shapes and sizes** relative to body size varied greatly between dinosaurs.

- **In many meat-eating dinosaurs** that ran on two back legs, the claws on the fingers were long and sharp, similar to a cat's claws.

- **A small, meat-eating dinosaur** such as *Troodon* probably used its finger claws for grabbing small mammals and lizards, and for scrabbling in the soil for insects and worms.

- **Larger meat-eating dinosaurs** such as *Allosaurus* may have used their hand claws to hold and slash their prey.

- **Huge plant-eating sauropods** such as *Diplodocus* had claws on its elephant like feet that resembled nails or hooves.

- **Many dinosaurs** had 5 clawed digits on their feet, but some, such as *Tyrannosaurus*, had only 3 clawed toes on each foot to support their weight.

- **Some of the largest dinosaur claws** belonged to *Deinocheirus* – its massive finger claws were more than 35 cm long.

- ***Deinocheirus*** was probably a gigantic ostrich-dinosaur that lived in the Late Cretaceous Period in Mongolia. Only parts of its fossil hands and arms have been found, so the rest of it remains a mystery.

◄ *The long, relatively sharp finger claws of* Troodon *were used for extracting small prey and for self defence.*

Asia

- **Hundreds of kinds of dinosaurs** have been discovered on the continent of Asia.

- **In Asia,** most of the dinosaur fossils that have been found so far were located in the Gobi Desert, in Central Asia, and in present-day China. Some were also found in present-day India.

- **Remains of the huge plant-eating sauropod** *Titanosaurus* were uncovered near Umrer, in central India.

- **Titanosaurus** was about 12 m long and weighed 5–10 tonnes.

- **Titanosaurus** lived about 70 million years ago, and was very similar in shape to its close

cousin of the same time, *Saltasaurus*, from South America.

- **Fossils** of the sauropod *Barapasaurus* were found in India. They date from the Early Jurassic Period, about 180 million years ago.

- **Barapasaurus** was 18 m long and probably weighed more than 20 tonnes.

- **Fossils** of the dinosaur *Dravidosaurus*, from the stegosaur group, were found near Tiruchirapalli in southern India.

- **Dravidosaurus** was about 3 m in total length. It lived much later than other stegosaurs, in the Late Cretaceous Period about 70 million years ago.

- **Dravidosaurus** had bony plates sticking up from its back, like *Stegosaurus*.

▲ *Dinosaur fossil finds span this vast continent.*

Coelophysis

- **Coelophysis** was a small, agile dinosaur that lived early in the Age of Dinosaurs, about 220 million years ago.

- **A huge collection of fossils** of *Coelophysis* was found in the late 1940s, at a place now known as Ghost Ranch, New Mexico, USA.

- **Hundreds** of *Coelophysis* were preserved together at Ghost Ranch – possibly a herd that drowned as the result of a sudden flood.

- **Coelophysis** was almost 3 m in total length.

- **The very slim, lightweight build** of *Coelophysis* meant that it probably weighed only 25–28 kg.

- **Coelophysis** belonged to the group of dinosaurs known as coelurosaurs. It probably ate small animals such as insects, worms and lizards.

- **Long, powerful back legs** allowed *Coelophysis* to run fast.

- **The front limbs** of *Coelophysis* were like arms, each with a hand bearing three large, strong, sharp-clawed fingers for grabbing prey.

- **Coelophysis** means 'hollow form'. It was so-named because some of its bones were hollow, like the bones of birds, making it lighter.

- **Coelophysis** had many small, sharp teeth in its narrow, birdlike skull.

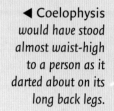

◀ Coelophysis would have stood almost waist-high to a person as it darted about on its long back legs.

Dinosaur fossil-hunters

- **Many dinosaurs** were found in the USA in the 1870s–90s by Othniel Charles Marsh and Edward Drinker Cope.

- **Marsh and Cope** were great rivals, each one trying to find bigger, better and more dinosaur fossils than the other.

- **The rivalry between Marsh and Cope** extended to bribing people to smash each other's fossils with hammers, planting fake fossils, and damaging food, water and other supplies at each other's camps in the Mid-West.

Edward Drinker Cope (1840-97) **Othniel Charles Marsh (1831-99)**

★ STAR FACT ★

One of the first great fossil-hunters in the USA was Joseph Leidy, who found *Troodon* in 1856.

- **Cope and Marsh found and described** about 130 new kinds of dinosaurs between 1877 and 1897.

- **Joseph Tyrrell** discovered fossils of *Albertosaurus* in 1884, in what became a very famous dinosaur region, the Red Deer River area of Alberta, Canada.

- **Lawrence Lambe** found and described many North American dinosaur fossils, such as *Centrosaurus* in 1904.

- **German fossil experts** Werner Janensch and Edwin Hennig led expeditions to east Africa in 1908–12, and discovered *Brachiosaurus* and *Kentrosaurus*.

- **From 1933** Yang Zhong-jiang (also called CC Young) led many fossil-hunting trips in various parts of China.

- **José Bonaparte** from Argentina has found many fossils in that region, including *Carnotaurus* in 1985.

Size

- **The biggest dinosaurs** were the sauropods such as *Brachiosaurus* and *Argentinosaurus* – but working out how heavy they were when they were alive is very difficult.

- *Brachiosaurus* is known from many remains, including almost complete skeletons, so its length can be measured accurately.

- **A dinosaur's weight** is estimated from a scaled-down model of its skeleton 'fleshed out' with muscles, guts and skin on the bones, using similar reptiles such as crocodiles for comparison.

- **The size of a dinosaur** model is measured by immersing it in water to find its volume.

- **The volume of a model dinosaur** is scaled up to find the volume of the real dinosaur when it was alive.

> ★ STAR FACT ★
> The weights and volumes of reptiles alive today are used to calculate the probable weight of a dinosaur when it was alive.

- **The sauropod** *Apatosaurus* is now well known from about 12 skeletons, which between them have almost every bone in its body.

- **Different experts** have 'fleshed out' the skeleton of *Apatosaurus* by different amounts, so estimates of its weight vary from 20 tonnes to more than 50 tonnes.

- **The length of** *Apatosaurus* is known accurately to have been 21 m in total.

- **Fossils of a dinosaur called** *Brontosaurus* were found to be identical to those of *Apatosaurus*, and since the name *Apatosaurus* had been given first, this was the name that had to be kept – so, officially, there is no dinosaur called *Brontosaurus*.

▲ It is thought that despite its massive size, *Apatosaurus* would have been able to trot surprisingly quickly on its relatively long legs.

Long neck allowed head to browse in treetops

Massive, heavy tail to swing at attackers

Human-sized meat-eaters present little threat

▶ Reconstruction of *Argentinosaurus* is based on relatively few of its own bones, combined with other bones from similar sauropod dinosaurs.

Heterodontosaurus

- **Heterodontosaurus** was a very small dinosaur at only 1.2 m in length (about as long as a large dog), and would have stood knee-high to a human.

- **Heterodontosaurus** lived about 205–195 million years ago, at the beginning of the Jurassic Period.

- **Probably standing partly upright** on its longer back legs, *Heterodontosaurus* would have been a fast runner.

- **Fossils** of *Heterodontosaurus* come from Lesotho in southern Africa and Cape Province in South Africa.

▶ *Tiny and slim, Heterodontosaurus looked outwardly similar to mini-meat-eaters such as Compsognathus.*

> ★ STAR FACT ★
> The name *Heterodontosaurus* means 'different-toothed reptile'.

- **Most dinosaurs had teeth of only one shape** in their jaws, but *Heterodontosaurus* had three types of teeth.

- **The front teeth** of *Heterodontosaurus* were small, sharp and found only in the upper jaw. They bit against the horny, beak-like lower front of the mouth.

- **The four middle teeth** of *Heterodontosaurus* were long and curved, similar to the tusks of a wild boar, and were perhaps used for fighting rivals or in self-defence.

- **The back or cheek teeth** of *Heterodontosaurus* were long and had sharp tops for chewing.

- **Heterodontosaurus** probably ate low-growing plants such as ferns.

Speed

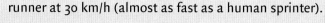

- **The fastest-running dinosaurs** had long, slim, muscular legs and small, lightweight bodies.

- **'Ostrich-dinosaurs'** were probably the speediest dinosaurs, perhaps attaining the same top speed as today's ostrich – 70 km/h.

- **The main leg muscles** of the ostrich-dinosaur *Struthiomimus* were in its hips and thighs.

- **The hip and leg design** of ostrich-dinosaurs meant that they could swing their limbs to and fro quickly, like those of a modern racehorse.

- **Large, powerful, plant-eating dinosaurs** such as the 'duck-bill' *Edmontosaurus* may have pounded along on their huge back legs at 40 km/h.

- **Plant-eaters** such as *Iguanodon* and *Muttaburrasaurus* may have trotted along at 10–12 km/h for many hours.

- **Some experts think** that the great meat-eater *Tyrannosaurus* may have been able to run at 50 km/h.

- **Other experts think** *Tyrannosaurus* was a relatively slow runner at 30 km/h (almost as fast as a human sprinter).

- **The slowest dinosaurs** were giant sauropods such as *Brachiosaurus*, which probably plodded at 4–6 km/h (about human walking speed).

- **Today's fastest runner**, the cheetah, would beat any dinosaur with its maximum burst of speed of more than 100 km/h.

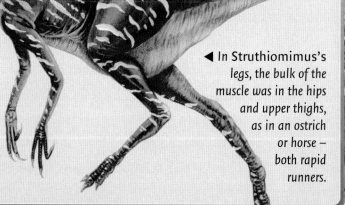

◀ *In Struthiomimus's legs, the bulk of the muscle was in the hips and upper thighs, as in an ostrich or horse – both rapid runners.*

Allosaurus

- **Allosaurus** was a huge meat-eating dinosaur, almost as big as *Tyrannosaurus*.

- **Allosaurus** was about 11–12 m in total length.

- **The weight** of *Allosaurus* is variously estimated at 1.5–4 tonnes.

- **The head** of *Allosaurus* was almost 1 m long, but its skull was light, with large gaps or 'windows' that would have been covered by muscle and skin.

- **Allosaurus** could not only open its jaws in a huge gape, but it could also flex them so that the whole mouth became wider, for an even bigger bite.

- **Allosaurus** lived about 155–135 million years ago, during the Late Jurassic and Early Cretaceous Periods.

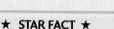

★ STAR FACT ★
The remains of 60 *Allosaurus* were found in the Cleveland-Lloyd Dinosaur Quarry, Utah, USA.

◀ *Allosaurus* almost rivalled *Tyrannosaurus* in size, but lived 70 million years earlier.

- **Most** *Allosaurus* fossils come from the states in the American Midwest.

- **Allosaurus** may have hunted the giant sauropod dinosaurs such as *Diplodocus*, *Camarasaurus* and *Brachiosaurus*.

- **Fossils** of *Allosaurus* were identified in Africa, and a smaller or 'dwarf' version was found in Australia.

Armour

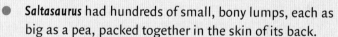

- **Many kinds of dinosaurs** had protective 'armour'.

- **Some armour** took the form of bony plates, or osteoderms, embedded in the skin.

- **A dinosaur with armour** might weigh twice as much as a same-sized dinosaur without armour.

- **Armoured dinosaurs** are divided into two main groups – the ankylosaurs and the nodosaurs.

- **The large sauropod** *Saltasaurus* had a kind of armour.

▶ Ankylosaurus's tail club was nearly 1 m across.

- **Saltasaurus** had hundreds of small, bony lumps, each as big as a pea, packed together in the skin of its back.

- **On its back**, *Saltasaurus* also had about 50 larger pieces of bone the size of a human hand.

- **Saltasaurus** is named after the Salta region of Argentina, where its fossils were found.

- **Uruguay** provided another site for *Saltasaurus* fossils.

- **Saltasaurus** was 12 m long and weighed about 3–4 tonnes.

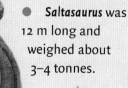

Carnotaurus

- **The big, powerful, meat-eating** *Carnotaurus* is in the carnosaur group of dinosaurs.

- *Carnotaurus* fossils come mainly from the Chubut region of Argentina, South America.

- *Carnotaurus* lived about 100 million years ago.

- **A medium-sized dinosaur**, *Carnotaurus* was about 7.5 m in total length and weighed up to 1 tonne.

- **The skull of** *Carnotaurus* was relatively tall from top to bottom and short from front to back, compared to other carnosaurs like *Allosaurus* and *Tyrannosaurus*, giving it a snub-snouted appearance.

- **The name** *Carnotaurus* means 'meat-eating bull', referring partly to its bull-like face.

- *Carnotaurus* had two curious, cone-shaped bony crests or 'horns', one above each eye, where the horns of a modern bull would be.

- **Rows of extra-large scales**, like small lumps, ran along *Carnotaurus* from its head to its tail.

- **Like** *Tyrannosaurus*, *Carnotaurus* had very small front limbs that could not reach its mouth, and may have had no use.

◀ *The fossils of Carnotaurus were first discovered in 1985.*

- *Carnotaurus* probably ate plant-eating dinosaurs such as *Chubutisaurus*, although its teeth and jaws were not especially big or strong.

Ankylosaurs

- **Ankylosaurs** had a protective armour of bony plates.

- **Unlike the armoured nodosaurs**, ankylosaurs had a large lump of bone at the ends of their tails, which they used as a hammer or club.

- **One of the best-known ankylosaurs**, from the preserved remains of about 40 individuals, is *Euoplocephalus*.

- **Euoplocephalus**, or 'well-armoured head', had bony shields on its head and body, and even had bony eyelids. Blunt spikes ran along its back.

- **The hefty** *Euoplocephalus* was about 7 m long and weighed 2 tonnes or more.

- *Euoplocephalus* lived about 75–70 million years ago in Alberta, Canada and Montana, USA.

- **Specimens of** *Euoplocephalus* are usually found singly, so it probably did not live in herds.

- **The ankylosaur** *Pinacosaurus* had bony nodules like chain-mail armour in its skin, and rows of blunt spikes from neck to tail.

- **Ankylosaurs** had small, weak teeth, and probably ate soft, low-growing ferns and horsetails.

▶ *Euoplocephalus probably cropped low plants with its beaklike mouth.*

> ★ **STAR FACT** ★
> *Pinacosaurus* was about 6 m long and lived in Asia some 80–75 million years ago.

Herbivores

- **Hundreds of kinds of dinosaurs** were herbivores, or plant-eaters. As time passed, the plants available for them to eat changed or evolved.

- **Early in the Age of Dinosaurs**, during the Triassic Period, the main plants for dinosaurs to eat were conifer trees, gingkoes, cycads and the smaller seed-ferns, ferns, horsetails and club-mosses.

- **A few cycads** are still found today. They resemble palm trees, with umbrella-like crowns of long green fronds on top of tall, unbranched, trunklike stems.

- **In the Triassic Period**, only prosauropod dinosaurs were big enough or had necks long enough to reach tall cycad fronds or gingko leaves.

- **In the Jurassic Period**, tall conifers such as redwoods and 'monkey-puzzle' trees became common.

- **The huge, long-necked sauropods** of the Jurassic Period would have been able to reach high into tall conifer trees to rake off their needles.

- **In the Middle Cretaceous Period**, a new type of plant food appeared – the flowering plants.

★ **STAR FACT** ★
Gingkoes are still found today in the form of the maidenhair tree, with fan-shaped leaves.

- **By the end of the Cretaceous Period** there were many flowering trees and shrubs, such as magnolias, maples and walnuts.

- **No dinosaurs ate grass**, because grasses did not appear on Earth until 30–20 million years ago, long after the dinosaurs had died out.

▼ During the warm, damp Jurassic Period, plants thrived in most areas, covering land that previously had been barren. Massive plant-eaters such as Barosaurus thrived on the high-level fronds, needles and leaves of towering tree-ferns, gingkoes and conifers.

Barosaurus, 26 m long and 25–30 tonnes

Triceratops

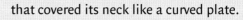

- **Many fossil remains** of *Triceratops* have been found. It is one of the most studied and best known dinosaurs.

- *Triceratops* was the largest of the plant-eating ceratopsians, or 'horn-faced' dinosaurs.

- *Triceratops* lived at the very end of the Age of Dinosaurs, 67–65 million years ago.

- **Fossils of 50 or so** *Triceratops* have been found in North America, though no complete skeleton has been found.

- *Triceratops* was about 9 m long and weighed 5–6 tonnes – as big as the largest elephants of today.

- **As well as a short nose horn** and two long eyebrow horns, *Triceratops* also had a wide, sweeping frill

- that covered its neck like a curved plate.

- **The neck frill** of *Triceratops* may have been an anchor for the dinosaur's powerful chewing muscles.

- **Acting as a shield**, the bony neck frill of *Triceratops* may have protected it as it faced predators head-on.

- *Triceratops'* neck frill may have been brightly coloured, to impress rivals or enemies.

- **The beak-like front** of *Triceratops'* mouth was toothless, but it had sharp teeth for chewing in its cheeks.

◄ The beak, head and neck frill of *Triceratops made up almost a quarter of its length.*

Earliest dinosaurs

- **The first known dinosaurs** appeared about 230–225 million years ago, in the Middle Triassic Period.

- **The earliest dinosaurs** were small-to-medium meat-eaters with sharp teeth and claws. They ran quickly on their two longer back legs.

- **Fossils** of *Herrerasaurus* date from 228 million years ago and were found near San Juan in Argentina, South America.

- *Herrerasaurus* was about 3 m in total length, and probably weighed some 90 kg.

▲ Staurikosaurus *was about 2 m in total length.*

- **At about the same time and in the same place** as *Herrerasaurus*, there lived a similar-shaped dinosaur named *Eoraptor*, at only 1.5 m long.

- **The name** *Eoraptor* means 'dawn plunderer' or 'early thief'.

- *Staurikosaurus* was a meat-eater similar to *Herrerasaurus*. It is known to have lived about the same time, in present-day Brazil, South America.

- *Procompsognathus* was another early meat-eater. It lived in the Late Triassic Period in Germany.

- *Pisanosaurus* lived in Argentina in the Late Triassic Period, and was only 1 m long. It may have been a plant-eater similar to *Lesothosaurus*.

★ STAR FACT ★
Eoraptor and *Herrerasaurus* hunted small animals such as lizards, insects and mammal-like reptiles.

Smallest dinosaurs

- **One of the smallest dinosaurs** was *Compsognathus*, which lived during the Late Jurassic Period, 155–150 million years ago.

- **Fossils** of *Compsognathus* come from Europe, especially southern Germany and southeastern France.

- *Compsognathus* was slim, with a long, narrow tail. It probably weighed less than 3 kg.

- **Each hand** of *Compsognathus* had two clawed fingers, and each foot had three long, clawed running toes, with another toe (the first or big toe) placed higher up in the 'ankle' region.

- *Compsognathus* had small teeth that were sharp and curved. It probably darted through the undergrowth

▼ *Very few fossils of Compsognathus have been found. They mainly belong to two individuals, one from Var, France, and the other from Bavaria, Germany. The larger specimen was about 1.2 m long, and was presumably an adult.*

★ STAR FACT ★
The little *Compsognathus* was only about 1 m long, and some specimens were even smaller, at 70 cm long.

after insects, spiders, worms and similar small prey.

- **Two other very small dinosaurs** were *Heterodontosaurus* and the 1-m long fabrosaur *Lesothosaurus*.

- **The smallest fossil dinosaur specimens** found to date are of *Mussaurus*, which means 'mouse reptile'.

- **Mussaurus** was a plant-eating prosauropod similar to *Plateosaurus*, which lived in the Late Triassic Period in South America.

- **The fossils of** *Mussaurus* measure just 20 cm long – but these are the fossils of babies, just hatched from their eggs. The babies would have grown into adults measuring 3 m long.

Africa

- **The first major discoveries** of dinosaur fossils in Africa were made from 1907, at Tendaguru in present-day Tanzania, east Africa.

- **Discoveries at Tendaguru** in east Africa included the giant sauropod *Brachiosaurus*, the smaller *Dicraeosaurus*, and the stegosaur-like *Kentrosaurus*.

- **Remains** of the massive sauropod *Cetiosaurus* were uncovered in Morocco, north Africa.

- ***Camarasaurus***, a 20-tonne plant-eater, is known from fossils found in Niger, as well as from European and North American fossils.

- **Fossils** of the huge, sail-backed meat-eater *Spinosaurus* come from Morocco and Egypt.

- **The sail-backed plant-eater**

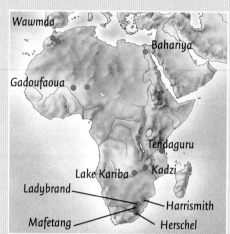

▲ In Africa, as elsewhere, fossils are easier to find in places with bare, rocky soils.

- *Ouranosaurus* is known from remains found in Niger.

- **Many sauropod fossils** were uncovered at sites in Zimbabwe, including *Barosaurus* and *Vulcanodon*.

- **Remains** of the medium-sized plant-eating prosauropod *Massospondylus* were extracted from several sites in southern Africa.

- **Fossils** thought to belong to the small prosauropod *Anchisaurus* were found in southern Africa, the only site for this dinosaur outside North America.

- **During the 1908–12 fossil-hunting expedition** to Tendaguru, more than 250 tonnes of fossil bones and rocks were carried by people for 65 km to the nearest port, for transport to Germany.

Mamenchisaurus

- *Mamenchisaurus* was a massive plant-eating dinosaur, a sauropod similar in appearance to *Diplodocus*.

- **The huge** *Mamenchisaurus* measured about 25 m from nose to tail tip.

- **The weight of** *Mamenchisaurus* has been estimated at 20–35 tonnes.

- *Mamenchisaurus* lived during the late Jurassic Period, from 160 to perhaps 140 million years ago.

- **The hugely long neck** of *Mamenchisaurus* had up to 19 vertebrae, or neckbones – more than almost any other dinosaur.

- *Mamenchisaurus* fossils were found in China.

- **The name** *Mamenchisaurus* is taken from the place where its fossils were discovered – Mamen Stream.

- *Mamenchisaurus* may be a close cousin of other sauropod dinosaurs found in the region, including *Euhelopus* and *Omeisaurus*.

- *Mamenchisaurus* may have stretched its vast neck high into trees to crop leaves, or – less likely – it may have lived in swamps and eaten soft water plants.

- *Mamenchisaurus* had the longest neck, at up to 15 m, of any dinosaur yet discovered.

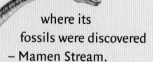

▲ The joints between the fossil bones of Mamenchisaurus's 15-m long neck show that the neck was not very flexible.

Deinonychus

- **Deinonychus** is one of the best-known members from the group of meat-eaters known as raptors.

- **The Middle Cretaceous Period**, about 115–100 million years ago, is when *Deinonychus* thrived.

- **Fossils** of *Deinonychus* come from the American

Midwest, mainly from Montana and Wyoming.

- **Deinonychus** was about 3 m long from nose to tail and weighed 60–70 kg, about the same as an adult human.

- **When remains of Deinonychus were dug up** and studied in the 1960s, they exploded the myth that dinosaurs were slow, small-brained and stupid.

- **Powerful, speedy and agile**, *Deinonychus* may have hunted in packs, like today's lions and wolves.

- **Deinonychus** had large hands with three powerful fingers, each tipped with a dangerous sharp claw.

- **On each foot**, *Deinonychus* had a massive, scythelike claw that it could flick in an arc to slice open prey.

- **The tail** of *Deinonychus* was stiff and could not be swished.

- **Deinonychus** and other similar dromaeosaurs, such as *Velociraptor*, were the basis for the cunning and terrifying raptors of the *Jurassic Park* films.

◀ *Deinonychus would often attack prey much larger than itself.*

Myths

- **Dinosaurs were the only animals alive** during the Age of Dinosaurs – false, there were many kinds of creatures, from worms, insects and fish to other kinds of reptiles.

- **Dinosaurs flew in the air** – false, although other reptiles called pterosaurs did fly.

- **Dinosaurs lived in the sea** – false, although other reptiles such as ichthyosaurs and plesiosaurs did.

- **Mammals appeared** on Earth after the dinosaurs died out – false. Small mammals lived all through the Age of Dinosaurs.

- **A single kind of dinosaur** survived all through the Age of Dinosaurs – false. A few

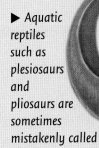

▶ Aquatic reptiles such as plesiosaurs and pliosaurs are sometimes mistakenly called 'dinosaurs'.

★ **STAR FACT** ★

Dinosaurs and humans fought each other – false. The last dinosaurs died out more than 60 million years before humans appeared.

---

kinds may have lived for 10, 20 or even 30 million years, but none came close to 160 million years.

- **Dinosaurs were huge lizards** – false. Dinosaurs were reptiles, but not members of the lizard group.

- **Dinosaurs gave birth to babies** – false. As far as we know, dinosaurs laid eggs.

- **All dinosaurs were green** – false, probably.

- **Dinosaurs live on today** – false …

… unless you've found one!

Reconstructions

- **No complete fossilized dinosaur**, with all its skin, muscles, guts and other soft parts, has yet been found.

- **Most dinosaurs are reconstructed** from the fossils of their hard parts – chiefly teeth, bones, horns and claws.

- **The vast majority of dinosaurs** are known from only a few fossil parts, such as several fragments of bones.

- **Fossil parts** of other, similar dinosaurs are often used in reconstructions to 'fill in' missing bones, teeth, and even missing heads, limbs or tails.

- **Soft body parts** from modern reptiles such as lizards are used as a guide for the reconstruction of a dinosaur's muscles and guts, which are added to the fossils.

- **On rare occasions**, remains are found of a dinosaur

> ★ STAR FACT ★
> 'Sue', the part-mummified *Tyrannosaurus*, was sold in 1997 for more than $8.3 million to the Field Museum, Chicago, USA.

body that dried out rapidly so that quite a few parts were preserved as mummified fossils.

- **One of the best-known**, part-mummified dinosaur fossils is 'Sue', a specimen of *Tyrannosaurus* found in 1990 in South Dakota, USA.

- **'Sue' is the biggest** and most complete preserved *Tyrannosaurus* ever found.

- **'Sue'** was a female *Tyrannosaurus*. It was named after its discoverer, fossil-hunter Susan Hendrickson of the Black Hills Institute of Geological Research.

▼ At a fossil site or 'dig', scientists record every stage of excavation with measurements, maps, photographs and sketches.

Frame supports upper body

Fossil 'bones' on display are usually lightweight copies in GRP (glass-reinforced plastic)

▶ Some fragile fossils are wrapped in plaster bandages. These harden to support and protect the remains so that they can be moved.

▶ This early reconstruction shows an ornithopod dinosaur similar to Iguanodon in a fairly upright, kangaroolike pose. As their knowledge increases, dinosaur experts change their views about how dinosaurs stood, walked and ran. Modern reconstructions tend to show Iguanodon on the move with its body almost horizontal.

Mini model shows fleshed-out appearance in life at much smaller scale

Male and female

- **In many living reptiles**, females are larger than males.

- **In dinosaur fossils**, the shapes of the hip bones and head crests can indicate if the creatures were male or female.

- **Head crest fossils** of different sizes and proportions belonging to the hadrosaur (duck-billed dinosaur) *Lambeosaurus* have been found.

- **Some** *Lambeosaurus* had short, rounded main crests with small, spikelike spurs pointing up and back.

- **Other** *Lambeosaurus* had a large, angular main crest with a large spur pointing up and back.

> ★ STAR FACT ★
> In *Parasaurolophus* specimens, some head crests were twice as long as others – probably a male-female difference.

- **The head crest differences** in *Lambeosaurus* fossils may indicate that males and females looked different.

- **Remains of the hadrosaur** *Corythosaurus* show two main sizes of head crest, perhaps one belonging to females and the other to males.

- **New studies** in the variations of head crests led to more than 8 different species of dinosaurs being reclassified as one species of *Corythosaurus*.

- **In dinosaurs and other animals**, differences between the sexes – either in size or specific features – is known as sexual dimorphism.

◀ *The large, angular head crest shows this is a male Corythosaurus.*

Herds

- **When the fossils of many individuals** of the same type are found together, there are various possible causes.

- **One reason why** individuals of the same dinosaur type are found preserved together is because their bodies were swept to the same place by a flood.

- **A group of individuals** of the same type may have died in the same place if they had lived there as a group.

- **There is much evidence** that various dinosaur types lived in groups or herds, examples being *Diplodocus*, *Triceratops* and *Iguanodon*.

- **Some fossil groups** include dinosaurs of different ages, from newly hatched babies to youngsters and adults.

- **Fossil footprints** suggest some dinosaurs lived in herds.

- **Footprints** of a plant-eating dinosaur were found with the prints of a meat-eater to one side of them – perhaps evidence of a hunter pursuing its victim.

▶ *A mixed-age herd would have left similar footprints of different sizes.*

> ★ STAR FACT ★
> At Peace River Canyon, British Columbia, Canada, some 1700 footprints were found.

- **Sometimes** the footprints of many dinosaurs of the same type are found together, suggesting a herd.

- **Sometimes larger footprints** are found to the sides of smaller ones, possibly indicating that adults guarded their young between them.

Stegosaurs

- **Stegosaurs** were a group of plant-eating dinosaurs that lived mainly during the Late Jurassic Period, 160–140 million years ago.

- **Stegosaurs are named after** the best-known of their group, *Stegosaurus*.

- **Stegosaurs are often called** 'plated dinosaurs', from the large, flat plates or slabs of bone on their backs.

- **Stegosaurs** probably first

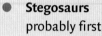

> ★ STAR FACT ★
> The back plates of *Kentrosaurus* were leaf- or diamond-shaped to about halfway along its back, and spike-shaped on its hips and tail.

appeared in eastern Asia, then spread to other continents, especially North America and Africa.

- **The stegosaur** *Kentrosaurus* was about 5 m long and weighed an estimated 1 tonne.

- **The name** *Kentrosaurus* means 'spiky reptile'.

- *Kentrosaurus* lived about 155–150 million years ago in east Africa.

- **Most stegosaurs had no teeth** at the fronts of their mouths, but had horny beaks, like those of birds, for snipping off leaves.

- **Most stegosaurs chewed** their food with small, ridged cheek teeth.

◀ The back plates of Kentrosaurus were taller and narrower than those of Stegosaurus.

Cousins: Air

- **Many flying creatures** lived during the Age of Dinosaurs, especially insects such as flies and dragonflies, and also birds.

- **The main flying reptiles** during the Age of Dinosaurs were the pterosaurs, or 'winged reptiles'.

- **Hundreds of different kinds** of pterosaurs came and went through almost the entire Age of Dinosaurs, about 220–65 million years ago.

- **The arms of a pterosaur** resembled wings – a light, thin, stretchy wing membrane was held out mainly by the finger bones, especially the fourth finger.

- **Pterosaurs** are sometimes called pterodactyls,

but *Pterodactylus* was just one kind of pterosaur.

- *Pterodactylus* had a wing span of 1–2 m. It lived 150–140 million years ago in southern Germany.

- **Some pterosaurs**, such as *Pterodactylus*, had very short tails, or no tail at all.

- **The pterosaur** *Rhamphorhynchus* had a long, trailing tail with a widened, paddle-shaped end.

- **Fossils** suggest that some pterosaurs, such as *Sordes*, had fur, and may have been warm-blooded, agile fliers rather than slow, clumsy gliders.

- **The biggest pterosaur**, and the largest flying animal ever, was *Quetzalcoatlus*. Its 'beak' was longer than an adult human, and its wings were almost 12 m across.

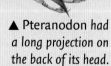

▲ Pteranodon had a long projection on the back of its head.

▶ The wings of Quetzalcoatlus were as long as those of a four-seater airplane.

Noses

- **Dinosaurs breathed** through their mouths and/or noses, like many other creatures today.

- **Fossil dinosaur skulls** show that there were two nose openings, called nares, in the bone.

- **A dinosaur's two nasal openings**, or nares, led to nasal chambers inside the skull, where the smell organs were located.

- **Some meat-eaters**, especially carnosaurs such as *Allosaurus* and *Tyrannosaurus*, had very large nasal chambers

▲ The nasal openings of Baryonyx were towards the front of its snout, rather than at the tip.

and probably had an excellent sense of smell.

- **In most dinosaurs** the nasal openings were at the front of the snout, just above the upper jaw.

- **In some dinosaurs**, especially sauropods such as *Mamenchisaurus* and *Brachiosaurus*, the nasal openings were higher on the skull, between the eyes.

- **Fossils** show that air passages led from the nasal chambers rearwards into the head for breathing.

- **The nasal openings** in a dinosaur's skull bone led to external openings, or nostrils, in the skin.

- **New evidence** from animals alive today suggests that a dinosaur's nostrils would have been lower down than the nares (the openings in the skull bone), towards the front of the snout.

Nests and eggs

▶ Most dinosaur eggs were elongated and had tough, flexible shells, like stiff leather.

- **There are hundreds of discoveries** of fossil dinosaur eggs and nests, found with the parent dinosaurs.

- **Eggs and nests** are known of the pig-sized plant-eater *Protoceratops*, an early kind of horned dinosaur.

- **Many** *Protoceratops*' nests were found in a small area, showing that these dinosaurs bred in colonies.

- *Protoceratops*' nests were shallow, bowl-shaped pits about 1 m across, scraped in the dry, sandy earth and surrounded by low walls.

- **At the** *Protoceratops* **site**, it was discovered that new nests had been made on top of old ones, showing that the colony was used again year after year.

- **The female** *Protoceratops* laid a clutch of 20 or so tough-

shelled, sausage-shaped eggs.

- *Protoceratops*' eggs were probably covered with earth and incubated by the heat of the sun.

- **Nests and eggs** of the small plant-eater *Orodromeus* have been found in Montana, USA.

- **In each nest** about 20 *Orodromeus* eggs were arranged neatly in a spiral, starting with one in the centre and working outwards.

- *Protoceratops* arranged its eggs neatly in its nest, in a circle or spiral shape resembling the spokes of a wheel.

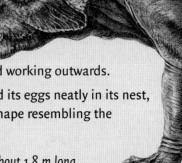

▶ Protoceratops was about 1.8 m long.

Names: 2

- **More than 100 kinds of dinosaurs** have been named after the people who first discovered their fossils, dug them up, or reconstructed the dinosaur.

- **The very large duck-bill (hadrosaur)** *Lambeosaurus* was named after Canadian fossil expert Lawrence Lambe.

- **Lawrence Lambe** worked mainly during the early 1900s, and named one of his finds *Stephanosaurus*.

- **In the 1920s**, *Stephanosaurus* was re-studied and renamed, along with *Didanodon*, as *Lambeosaurus*, in honour of Lambe's great work.

- **The full name** of the 'heavy-claw' meat-

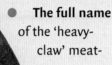

▲ The first fossil find of Baryonyx *was its huge thumb claw.*

★ STAR FACT ★
Australian *Leaellynasaura* was named after Lea Ellyn, the daughter of its discoverers.

eater *Baryonyx* is *Baryonyx walkeri*, after Bill Walker, the discoverer of its massive claw.

- **Part-time fossil-hunter** Bill Walker found the claw of *Baryonyx* in a clay pit quarry in Surrey, England.

- **Some dinosaur names** are quite technical, such as *Diplodocus*, which means 'double beam' – it was named for its tail bones, which have two long projections like a pair of skis.

- **The 4-m long plant-eater** *Othnielia*, related to *Hypsilophodon*, was named after the late 19th-century American fossil-hunter Othniel Charles Marsh.

- ***Parksosaurus***, a 2.5-m long plant-eater related to *Hypsilophodon*, was named in honour of Canadian dinosaur expert William Parks.

Diplodocus

- ***Diplodocus*** was a huge plant-eating dinosaur belonging to the group known as the sauropods.

- ***Diplodocus*** lived during the Late Jurassic Period, about 155–145 million years ago.

- **The first discovery** of *Diplodocus* fossils was in 1877, near Canyon City, Colorado, USA.

- **The main fossils** of *Diplodocus* were found in the Midwest of the USA, in Colorado, Utah and Wyoming.

- **At an incredible 27 m** or more in length, *Diplodocus* is one of the longest dinosaurs known.

- **Although so long**, *Diplodocus* was quite lightly built – it probably weighed 'only' 10–12 tonnes!

- ***Diplodocus*** probably swung its tiny head on its enormous neck to reach fronds and foliage in the trees.

- **The teeth** of *Diplodocus* were slim rods that formed a comblike fringe only around the front of its mouth.

- ***Diplodocus*** may have used its comblike teeth to strip leaves from twigs and swallow them without chewing.

- ***Diplodocus's*** nostrils were so high on its skull (almost above its eyes) that experts once thought it had a trunk like an elephant's.

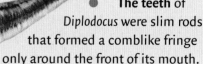

▶ Diplodocus *was long but light for a sauropod, weighing 'only' about 10 tonnes.*

Colours

- **No one knows** for certain what colours dinosaurs were.

- **There are several good fossil specimens** of dinosaur skin, but all of them are stone coloured, because fossils are living things that have turned to stone.

- **Some experts believe** that dinosaurs were similar in colour to crocodiles – dull greens and browns.

- **Dinosaurs** that were dull greens and browns would have been well camouflaged among trees, rocks and earth.

- **According to some experts**, certain dinosaurs may have been bright yellow, red or blue, and possibly striped or patched, like some of today's lizards and snakes.

- **Some dinosaurs** may have been brightly coloured to frighten off predators or to intimidate rivals at breeding time.

- **The tall 'sails'** of skin on the backs of the plant-eater *Ouranosaurus* and the meat-eater *Spinosaurus* may have been for visual display, as well as for (or instead of) temperature control.

- **The large, bony back plates** on stegosaurs may have been used for colourful displays to rivals.

- **The large neck frills** of horned dinosaurs such as *Triceratops* were possibly very colourful and used for display.

- **Recent finds** of dinosaur skin and scales with microscopic ridges and patterns on their surface may show how the scales reflected light, and so what colour they would have appeared.

◀ Like all reconstructions from fossils, the colours of featherered dinosaur *Caudipteryx* are intelligent guesswork.

Ornitholestes

- **Ornitholestes** was a smallish meat-eating dinosaur in the group known as coelurosaurs.

- **The name** *Ornitholestes* means 'bird robber' – experts who studied its fossils in the early 1900s imagined it chasing and killing the earliest birds.

- **Ornitholestes** lived about 150 million years ago, at the same time as the first birds.

- **Present-day Wyoming, USA,** was the home of *Ornitholestes*, a continent away from the earliest birds in Europe.

- **Only one specimen** of *Ornitholestes* has been found, along with parts of a hand at another site.

- **Ornitholestes** was about 2 m long from nose to tail-tip.

> ★ STAR FACT ★
> According to some experts, *Ornitholestes* may have had a slight ridge or crest on its nose. Other experts disagree.

- **Slim and lightweight**, *Ornitholestes* probably weighed only about 12–15 kg.

- **The teeth** of *Ornitholestes* were small and well-spaced, but also slim and sharp, well suited to grabbing small animals for food.

- **Ornitholestes** had very strong arms and hands, and powerful fingers with long claws, ideal for grabbing baby dinosaurs newly hatched from their eggs.

◀ Ornitholestes relied for survival on speed and its good senses of sight and smell.

Duck-bills

- **'Duck-bills'** is the common name for the group of dinosaurs called hadrosaurs.

- **Hadrosaurs were big plant-eaters** that walked mainly on their two large, powerful rear legs.

- **Hadrosaurs** were one of the last main dinosaur groups to appear on Earth, less than 100 million years ago.

- **Hadrosaurs were named after** *Hadrosaurus*, the first dinosaur of the group to be discovered as fossils, found in 1858 in New Jersey, USA.

- **Most hadrosaurs had wide mouths** that were flattened and toothless at the front, like a duck's beak.

- **Huge numbers of cheek teeth** filled the back of the hadrosaur's mouth, arranged in rows called batteries. They were ideal for chewing tough plant food.

- **Some hadrosaurs** had tall, elaborate crests or projections of bone on their heads, notably *Corythosaurus*, *Tsintaosaurus*, *Saurolophus* and *Parasaurolophus*.

- **Hadrosaurs that lacked bony crests** and had low, smooth heads included *Anatosaurus*, *Bactrosaurus*, *Kritosaurus* and *Edmontosaurus*.

- **The name** *Hadrosaurus* means 'big reptile'.

▶ Parasaurolophus *may have had a 'web' of brightly coloured skin extending from its bony head crest to the back of its neck – perhaps part of a visual display for mating, herd dominance or gaining territory. Alternatively, the bony crest may have lacked skin and simply projected upwards and backwards like a pole.*

Possible inflatable bag of skin on snout and forehead

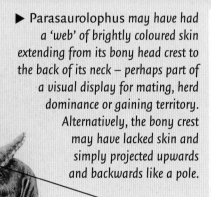

Tall, relatively narrow tail with muscular tail base to swish tail from side to side

▲ Asian *Saurolophus* was about 12 m long – larger than its North American counterparts. It also had a relatively larger, horn-like head crest, which may have supported a balloon-like pouch of skin that the dinosaur could inflate to make a trumpeting call.

Powerful rear legs for rapid walking and trotting

★ **STAR FACT** ★
Edmontosaurus may have had a loose bag of skin on its nose that it blew up like a balloon to make a honking or trumpeting noise – perhaps a breeding call.

Warm or cold blood?

- **If dinosaurs were cold-blooded** and obtained heat only from their surroundings, like reptiles today, they would have been slow or inactive in cold conditions.

- **If dinosaurs were warm-blooded**, like birds and mammals today, they would have been able to stay warm and active in cold conditions.

- **Some time ago** experts believed that all dinosaurs were cold-blooded, but today there is much disagreement.

- **One type of evidence** for warm-bloodedness comes from the detailed structure of the insides of very well-preserved fossil bones.

- **The inside structure** of some fossil dinosaur bones is more like that of warm-blooded creatures than reptiles.

▲ The detailed microscopic structure inside bones can give clues as to warm- or cold-bloodedness.

- **Certain small, meat-eating dinosaurs** may have evolved into birds, and since birds are warm-blooded, these dinosaurs may have been, too.

- **In a 'snapshot' count** of dinosaur fossils, the number of predators compared to prey is more like that in mammals than in reptiles.

- **Some dinosaurs** were thought to live in herds and raise families, as many birds and mammals do today. In reptiles, such behaviour is rare.

- **Most dinosaurs stood upright** on straight legs, a posture common to warm-blooded creatures, but not to other, cold-blooded reptiles.

- **If dinosaurs had been warm-blooded**, they would probably have needed to eat at least 10 times more food than if they were cold-blooded, to 'burn' food energy and make heat.

Eustreptospondylus

- **Eustreptospondylus was** a large meat-eater that lived in present-day Oxfordshire and Buckinghamshire, in central southern England.

- **Eustreptospondylus** lived about 165 million years ago.

- **In the 1850s**, a fairly complete skeleton of a young Eustreptospondylus was found near Wolvercote, Oxford, but was named as Megalosaurus, the only other big meat-eater known from the region.

- **In 1964**, British fossil expert Alick Walker showed that the Wolvercote dinosaur was not Megalosaurus, and gave it a new name, Eustreptospondylus.

- **Eustreptospondylus** means 'well curved, or true reversed, backbone'.

- **A full-grown** Eustreptospondylus measured about 7 m in total length.

- **Eustreptospondylus** is estimated to have weighed a massive 200–250 kg.

- **In its enormous mouth**, Eustreptospondylus had a great number of small, sharp teeth.

- **Eustreptospondylus** may have hunted sauropods such as Cetiosaurus and stegosaurs, two groups that roamed the region at the time.

◄ Eustreptospondylus weighed about the same as a very large lion today, and was doubtless just as deadly.

★ STAR FACT ★
For more than 100 years, the fossil Eustreptospondylus from near Oxford was known by the name Megalosaurus.

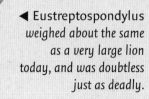

Pachycephalosaurs

- **The pachycephalosaurs** are named after one of the best-known members of the group, *Pachycephalosaurus.*

- *Pachycephalosaurus* means 'thick-headed reptile', due to the domed and hugely thickened bone on the top of its skull – like a cyclist's crash helmet.

  - **Pachycephalosaurs** were one of the last dinosaur groups to thrive. They lived 75–65 million years ago.

Extra thick skull bone

◀ Typical of its group, Pachycephalosaurus had a thickened layer of bone on the top of its head.

> ★ **STAR FACT** ★
> Pachycephalosaurs are often known as the 'bone-heads' or 'helmet-heads'.

- **Pachycephalosaurs were plant-eaters** that stood up and ran on their longer back legs.

- *Pachycephalosaurus* was about 4.5 m long from nose to tail, and lived in the American Midwest.

- *Stegoceras*, also from the American Midwest, was about 2.5 m long with a body the size of a goat.

- *Homalocephale*, another pachycephalosaur, was about 3 m long and had a flatter skull. It lived in east Asia.

  - **Pachycephalosaurs** may have defended themselves by lowering their heads and charging at their enemies.

  - **At breeding time**, the males may have engaged in head-butting contests, as some sheep and goats do today.

Baryonyx

- **Baryonyx** was a large meat-eating dinosaur that lived about 120 million years ago.

- **The first fossil find** of *Baryonyx* was its huge thumb claw, discovered in Surrey, England, in 1983.

- **The total length** of *Baryonyx* was 10–11 m.

- **Baryonyx** had a slim shape and long, narrow tail, and probably weighed less than 2 tonnes.

- **The head** of *Baryonyx*

▶ Fossils of Baryonyx were found associated with remains of fish scales, suggesting this dinosaur was a semi-aquatic fish-catcher.

was unusual for a meat-eating dinosaur in having a very long, narrow snout, similar to today's slim-snouted crocodiles.

- **The teeth** of *Baryonyx* were long and slim, especially at the front of its mouth.

  - **The general similarities** between *Baryonyx* and a crocodile suggest that *Baryonyx* may have been a fish-eater.

  - **Baryonyx** may have lurked in swamps or close to rivers, darting its head forwards on its long, flexible neck to snatch fish.

  - **The massive thumb claw** of *Baryonyx* may have been used to hook fish or amphibians from the water.

  - **The long thumb claw** of *Baryonyx* measured about 35 cm in length.

Footprints

- **Thousands of fossilized dinosaur footprints** have been found all over the world.

- **Some dinosaurs left footprints** when they walked on the soft mud or sand of riverbanks. Then the mud baked hard in the sun, and was covered by more sand or mud, which helped preserve the footprints as fossils.

- **Some fossil footprints** were made when dinosaur feet left impressions in soft mud or sand that was then

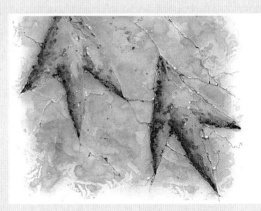

◀ The relative positions of footprints indicate how a dinosaur stood or moved.

> ★ STAR FACT ★
> Hadrosaur footprints 135 cm long and 80 cm wide were found near Salt Lake City, Utah, USA.

covered by volcanic ash, which set hard.

- **Many footprints** have been found together in lines, called 'trackways'. These suggest that some dinosaurs lived in groups, or used the same routes regularly.

- **The distance between same-sized footprints** indicates whether a dinosaur was walking, trotting or running.

- **Footprints of big meat-eaters** such as *Tyrannosaurus* show 3 toes with claws, on a forward-facing foot.

- **In big plant-eaters** such as *Iguanodon*, each footprint shows 3 separate toes, but less or no claw impressions, and the feet point slightly inwards.

- **In giant plant-eating sauropods**, each footprint is rounded and has indentations of nail-like 'hooves'.

- **Some sauropod footprints** are more than 1 m across.

Archosaurs

- **Archosaurs** were a very large group of reptiles that included the dinosaurs as one of their subgroups.

- **Other archosaur subgroups** included thecodonts, flying reptiles called pterosaurs, and crocodiles.

- **The thecodonts** included a smaller reptile group, the ornithosuchians – possibly the dinosaurs' ancestors.

- **One of the most dinosaur-like of the archosaurs** was the thecodont *Ornithosuchus*.

- **The 4-m long** *Ornithosuchus* stood almost upright.

- **Ornithosuchus** fossils were found in Scotland.

- **Sharp-toothed** *Ornithosuchus* was probably a powerful predator.

▶ *Ornithosuchus had a mix of features, both non-dinosaur (hips, back plates) and dinosaur (legs, skull).*

- **Features** in *Ornithosuchus's* backbone, hips and feet indicate that it was almost certainly not a dinosaur.

- **The archosaur** *Longisquama* was a lizard-like reptile only 15 cm long, with tall scales forming a V-shaped row along its back.

- **Archosaur means 'ruling reptile'**, and archosaurs did indeed rule the land, swamps and skies for over 170 million years.

Teeth

- **Some of most common fossil remains** of dinosaurs are their teeth – the hardest parts of their bodies.

- **Dinosaur teeth** come in a huge range of sizes and shapes – daggers, knives, shears, pegs, combs, rakes, filelike rasps, crushing batteries and vices.

- **In some dinosaurs**, up to three-quarters of a tooth was fixed into the jaw bone, so only one-quarter showed.

- **The teeth of plant-eaters** such as *Iguanodon* had angled tops that rubbed past each other in a grinding motion.

- **Some duck-bill dinosaurs** (hadrosaurs) had

★ STAR FACT ★
Troodon, or 'wounding tooth', was named on the evidence of just 1 or 2 teeth.

more than 1000 teeth, all at the back of the mouth.

- **Like modern reptiles**, dinosaurs probably grew new teeth to replace old, worn or broken ones.

- **Individual teeth** were replaced at different times.

- **Some of the largest teeth** of any dinosaur belonged to 9-m long *Daspletosaurus*, a tyrannosaurlike meat-eater.

- **Some of** *Daspletosaurus*'s teeth were 18 cm long.

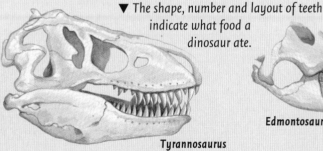

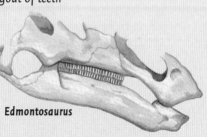

▼ The shape, number and layout of teeth indicate what food a dinosaur ate.

Tyrannosaurus

Edmontosaurus

Apatosaurus

Plateosaurus

- **Plateosaurus**, a prosauropod, was one of the first really big dinosaurs to appear, some 220 million years ago.

- **The name** *Plateosaurus* means 'flat reptile'.

- **Groups of** *Plateosaurus* have been found at various sites, including one in Germany and one in France.

- **Plateosaurus** used its many small, serrated teeth to crop and chew plant food.

- **Plateosaurus** had very flexible, clawed fingers, which it perhaps used to pull branches of food to its mouth.

- **Plateosaurus** could bend its fingers 'backwards', allowing it to walk on its hands and fingers, in the same posture as its feet and toes.

- **Plateosaurus's thumbs** had especially large, sharp claws, perhaps used as weapons to jab and stab enemies.

- **Fossil experts** once thought that *Plateosaurus* dragged its tail as it walked.

- **Experts today** suggest that *Plateosaurus* carried its tail off the ground, to act as a balance to its head, long neck and the front part of its body.

- **Plateosaurus** was one of the earliest dinosaurs to be officially named, in 1837, even before the term 'dinosaur' had been invented.

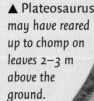

▲ Plateosaurus may have reared up to chomp on leaves 2–3 m above the ground.

Growth and age

- **No one knows for sure** how fast dinosaurs grew, how long they took to reach full size, or how long they lived.

- **Most estimates** of dinosaur growth rates and ages come from comparisons with today's reptiles.

- **Some reptiles today** continue to grow throughout their lives, although their growth rate slows with age.

- **Dinosaurs** may have grown fast as youngsters and slower as adults, never quite stopping until they died.

- **Estimates for the age of a full-grown meat-eater** such as *Tyrannosaurus* range from 20 to more than 50 years.

- **Full-grown, small meat-eaters** such as *Compsognathus* may have lived to be only 3–10 years old.

- **A giant sauropod** probably lived to be 50 years old, or even over 100 years old.

- **Like many reptiles today**, a dinosaur's growth rate probably depended largely on its food supply.

- **Dinosaurs** probably ate a lot and grew fast when food was plentiful, and slowed down when food was scarce.

- **During its lifetime**, a big sauropod such as *Brachiosaurus* would have increased its weight 2000 times (compared to 20 times in a human).

▶ Tyrannosaurus *may have taken 20–50 years to reach adult size.*

Cousins: Land

◀ Protosuchus, *a North American crocodile, lived 200 million years ago.*

- **The first mammals** appeared on Earth at about the same time as the early dinosaurs.

- **Various kinds of mammals** survived all through the Age of Dinosaurs, although none grew larger than a pet cat.

- **One of the first mammals** known from fossils is *Megazostrodon*, which resembled a shrew of today.

- **Land animals** during the Age of Dinosaurs included insects, spiders, other reptiles, birds and mammals.

- **Dinosaurs** had many large, fierce, reptile enemies.

- **One of the biggest** non-dinosaur land reptiles was *Deinosuchus* (or *Phobosuchus*), a type of crocodile.

- **Deinosuchus** lived in the Late Cretaceous Period, in present-day Texas, USA.

- **The fossil skull** of *Deinosuchus* measures about 2 m long, much bigger than any crocodile of today.

- **Megazostrodon** was just 12 cm long and its fossils, from 220–210 million years ago, come from southern Africa.

- **If Deinosuchus's body** was in proportion to its skull, it would have been 15 m long!

▶ Megazostrodon *probably fed like the shrews of today.*

Anchisaurus

- **Anchisaurus** was a prosauropod, a plant-eater with a small head, long neck and long tail.

- **Although officially named as a dinosaur** in 1912, *Anchisaurus* had in fact been discovered almost 100 years earlier.

- **Anchisaurus** was very small and slim compared to other prosauropods, with a body about the size of a large dog.

- **Fossils** of *Anchisaurus* date from the Early Jurassic times.

- **The remains of** *Anchisaurus* were found in Connecticut and Massachusetts, eastern USA, and in southern Africa.

- **With its small, serrated teeth,** *Anchisaurus* probably bit off the soft leaves of low-growing plants.

- **To reach leaves** on higher branches, *Anchisaurus* may

★ **STAR FACT** ★
Remains of Anchisaurus were the first fossils of a dinosaur to be discovered in North America in 1818.

have been able to rear up on its back legs.

- **Anchisaurus** had a large, curved claw on each thumb.

- **The thumb claws** of *Anchisaurus* may have been used as hooks to pull leafy branches towards the mouth, and/or as weapons for lashing out at enemies and inflicting wounds.

◀ *The main body of Anchisaurus was about the size of a pet dog such as a labrador.*

Cousins: Sea

- **Placodont reptiles** lived mainly during the Triassic Period. They were shaped like large salamanders or turtles, and probably ate shellfish.

- **The placodont** *Placodus* was about 2 m long and looked like a large, scaly newt.

- **The nothosaurs** were fish-eating reptiles of the Triassic Period. They had small heads, long necks and tails, and 4 flipper-shaped limbs.

- **Fossils** of the 3-m long nothosaur *Nothosaurus* have been found across Europe, Asia and Africa.

▼ *Plesiosaurus was 2.5 m long, and was one of many plesiosaurs to thrive in Jurassic seas.*

- **The dolphin-like ichthyosaur reptiles** had back fins, two-lobed tails and flipper-shaped limbs.

- **Many kinds of ichthyosaurs** thrived in the seas during the Triassic and Jurassic Periods, although they had faded away by the middle of the Cretaceous Period.

- **One of the biggest ichthyosaurs** was *Shonisaurus*, which measured up to 15 m long.

- **The plesiosaurs** were fish-eating reptiles of the Mesozoic Era, with small heads, tubby bodies, 4 flipper-shaped limbs and short, tapering tails.

- **The plesiosaur** *Elasmosaurus* was up to 14 m long, with more than half of this length being its extraordinarily long, snakelike neck.

★ **STAR FACT** ★
One of the biggest meat-eaters ever was the short-necked plesiosaur Liopleurodon, at possibly 20 m long and weighing 50 tonnes.

Dino-birds: 1

- **The earliest known bird** for which there is good fossil evidence, and which lived during the Age of Dinosaurs, is *Archaeopteryx*.

- ***Archaeopteryx*** lived in Europe during the Late Jurassic Period, about 155–150 million years ago.

- **At about 60 cm long** from nose to tail-tip, *Archaeopteryx* was about the size of a large crow.

- ***Archaeopteryx*** resembled a small, meat-eating dinosaur in many of its features, such as the teeth in its long, beaklike mouth, and its long, bony tail.

> ★ **STAR FACT** ★
> *Archaeopteryx* was covered with feathers that had the same detailed designs found in feathers covering flying birds today.

- **In 1951**, a fossilized part-skeleton was identified as belonging to a small dinosaur similar to *Compsognathus*, but in the 1970s it was re-studied and named *Archaeopteryx* – showing how similar the two creatures were.

- **Three clawed fingers** grew halfway along the front of each of *Archaeopteryx*'s wing-shaped front limbs.

- **The flying muscles** of *Archaeopteryx* were anchored to its large breastbone.

- ***Archaeopteryx*** probably flew, but not as fast or as skilfully as today's birds.

- ***Archaeopteryx*** probably fed by swooping on prey, running to catch small creatures such as insects and worms, or perhaps even by scavenging carrion.

Long tail with tail backbones

Three clawed 'fingers' midway along front of wing

Teeth in long, light jaws (all birds lack teeth today)

Flight feathers suited to agile manoeuvres in the air

▲ *Archaeopteryx* could probably glide well, swoop and turn as it pursued flying prey such as dragonflies. However, its long, strong legs suggest that it was also an able walker and runner. So it may have chased victims such as baby lizards and cockroaches on the ground.

Skin

- **Several fossils of dinosaur skin** have been found, revealing that dinosaurs had scales, like today's reptiles.

- **As in crocodiles**, the scales of a dinosaur were embedded in its thick, tough, leathery hide, rather than lying on top of its skin and overlapping, as in snakes.

- **When the first fossils** of dinosaur skin were found in the mid 1800s, scientists thought they were from giant prehistoric crocodiles.

- **Fossil skin** of the horned dinosaur *Chasmosaurus* has been found.

- **Chasmosaurus** had larger bumps or lumps, called tubercles, scattered among its normal-sized scales.

- **Samples of fossil skin** belonging to the

▶ Fossil skin, such as this piece from Edmontosaurus, is a relatively rare find.

★ STAR FACT ★
Many dinosaur scales were roughly six-sided, like the cells in a bee's honeycomb.

duck-bill hadrosaur *Edmontosaurus* have been found.

- **Edmontosaurus** was covered in thousands of small scales, like little pebbles, with larger lumps or tubercles spaced among them.

- **Various specimens** of fossil skin show that the scales of *Iguanodon*-type dinosaurs were larger than those of same-sized, similar duck-bill dinosaurs.

- **Scaly skin** protected a dinosaur against the teeth and claws of enemies, accidental scrapes, and the bites of small pests such as mosquitoes and fleas.

Camarasaurus

- **Camarasaurus** is one of the best known of all big dinosaurs, because so many almost-complete fossil skeletons have been found.

- **Camarasaurus** was a giant plant-eating sauropod.

- **Camarasaurus** lived during the Late Jurassic Period, about 155–150 million years ago.

- **The famous American fossil-hunter** Edward

◀ Compared to other sauropods, Camarasaurus had a short neck and tail.

Drinker Cope gave *Camarasaurus* its name in 1877.

- **The name** *Camarasaurus* means 'chambered reptile', because its backbones, or vertebrae, had large, scoop-shaped spaces in them, making them lighter.

- **The huge** *Camarasaurus* was about 18 m long.

- **Compared to other sauropods**, such as *Diplodocus*, *Camarasaurus* had a relatively short neck and tail, but a very bulky, powerful body and legs.

- **North America, Europe and Africa** were home to *Camarasaurus*.

- **A large, short-snouted, tall head**, like that of *Brachiosaurus*, characterized *Camarasaurus*.

- **A fossil skeleton** of a young *Camarasaurus* was uncovered in the 1920s, and had nearly every bone in its body lying in the correct position, as they were in life – an amazingly rare find.

Could dinosaurs live again?

- **The Jurassic Park movies** showed dinosaurs being recreated as living creatures in the modern world.

- **The instructions**, or genes, of all animals, including dinosaurs, are in the form of the genetic substance known as DNA (de-oxyribonucleic acid).

- **In Jurassic Park**, dinosaur DNA came not from dinosaur fossils, but from mosquitoes that had sucked the blood of living dinosaurs, and then been preserved.

- **Scientists** in Jurassic Park combined the DNA of dinosaurs with DNA from living amphibians such as frogs.

- **Tiny bits of DNA** have been recovered from fossils formed in the Age of Dinosaurs.

- **The bits of dinosaur DNA found so far** represent a tiny amount of the DNA needed to recreate a living thing.

- **Most scientists** doubt that living dinosaurs could really be made from bits of fossilized DNA.

- **Plants today** might not be suited to 'modern' dinosaurs.

- **'Modern' dinosaurs** might die from today's diseases.

- **The task of recreating** a living dinosaur from tiny fragments of DNA has been compared to writing all the plays of Shakespeare starting with couple of words.

◀ The heroes of Jurassic Park find a sick Triceratops.

Oviraptor

- **Oviraptor** was an unusual meat-eater from the dinosaur group known as theropods.

- **Fossils of** Oviraptor were found in the Omnogov region of the Gobi Desert in Central Asia.

- **From beak to tail-tip**, Oviraptor was about 2 m long.

- **Oviraptor** lived during the Late Cretaceous Period about 85–75 million years ago.

- **Oviraptor** was named 'egg thief' because the first of its fossils was found lying among the broken eggs possibly of another dinosaur Protoceratops.

- **The mouth of** Oviraptor had no teeth. Instead, it had a strong, curved beak, like that of a parrot or eagle.

- **On its forehead**, Oviraptor had a tall, rounded piece of bone, like a crest or helmet, sticking up in front of its eyes.

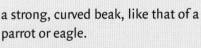

- **Oviraptor's** bony head crest resembled that of today's flightless bird, the cassowary.

- **Oviraptor** may have eaten eggs, or cracked open shellfish with its powerful beak.

◀ Oviraptor's unusual features included its parrot-like beak.

> **★ STAR FACT ★**
> Oviraptor had two bony spikes inside its mouth that it may have used to crack eggs when it closed its jaws.

Pack-hunters

- **Dinosaurs were reptiles**, but no reptiles today hunt in packs in which members cooperate with each other.

- **Certain types of crocodiles and alligators** come together to feed where prey is abundant, but they do not coordinate their attacks.

- **Fossil evidence** suggests that several kinds of meat-eating dinosaurs hunted in groups or packs.

- **Sometimes** the fossils of several individuals of the same type of dinosaur have been found in one place, suggesting the dinosaurs were pack animals.

- **The fossil bones** of some plant-eating dinosaurs have been found with many tooth marks on them, apparently made by different-sized predators, which may have hunted in packs.

- **Tyrannosaurus** may have been a pack-hunter.

- **In southwest Montana, USA**, the remains of three or four *Deinonychus* were found near the fossils of a much larger plant-eater named *Tenontosaurus*.

- **One** *Deinonychus* probably would not have attacked a full-grown *Tenontosaurus*, but a group of three or four might have.

◄ *The raptors could probably hunt alone, but also bring down larger prey in packs, as hyaenas or lions do today.*

> ★ STAR FACT ★
> Some meat-eaters may have had fairly large brains, enabling them to hunt as a group.

Ceratopsians

- **Ceratopsians** were large plant-eaters that appeared less than 90 million years ago.

- **Most ceratopsian fossils** come from North America.

- **'Ceratopsian' means 'horn-face'**, after the long horns on their snouts, eyebrows or foreheads.

- **Most ceratopsians** had a neck shield or frill that swept sideways and up from the back of the head to cover the upper neck and shoulders.

- **Well-known ceratopsians** included *Triceratops*, *Styracosaurus*, *Centrosaurus*, *Pentaceratops*, *Anchiceratops*, *Chasmosaurus* and *Torosaurus*.

- **The neck frills of some ceratopsians**, such as that of *Chasmosaurus*, had large gaps or 'windows' in the bone.

- **In life**, the windows in the neck frill of a ceratopsian were covered with thick, scaly skin.

- **Ceratopsians** had no teeth in the fronts of their hooked, beaklike mouths.

- **Using rows of powerful cheek teeth**, ceratopsians sheared their plant food.

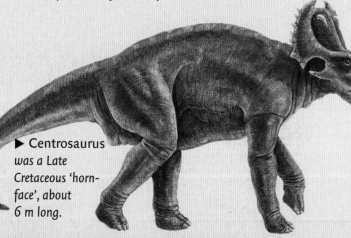

▶ Centrosaurus *was a Late Cretaceous 'horn-face', about 6 m long.*

> ★ STAR FACT ★
> *Torosaurus* had the longest skull of any land animal ever, at about 2.5 m from the front of the snout to the rear of the neck frill.

Babies

- **As far as we know,** female dinosaurs laid eggs, from which their babies hatched.

- **The time between** eggs being laid and babies hatching out is called the incubation period.

- **Incubation periods** for dinosaur eggs probably varied by weeks or months depending on the temperature, as in today's reptiles.

- **Many fossils** of adult *Maiasaura* (a duck-bill dinosaur, or hadrosaur) have been found, together with its nests, eggs and hatchlings (just-hatched babies).

- **Fossils of** *Maiasaura* come mainly from Montana, USA.

- **The name** *Maiasaura* means 'good mother reptile'.

- **The teeth of** *Maiasaura* babies found in the nest are slightly worn, showing that they had eaten food.

- **The leg bones and joints** of the *Maiasaura* babies were not quite fully formed, showing that they were not yet able to move about to gather their own food.

- **Evidence** from *Maiasaura* and other nesting sites shows that dinosaurs may have been caring parents, protecting and feeding their young.

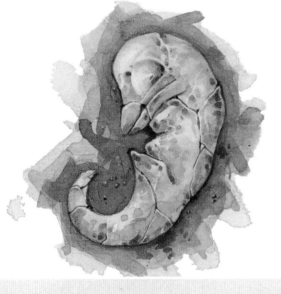

▲ Some fossil dinosaur eggs contain preserved embryos, still in the process of development. They use nutrients stored as egg yolk. Dinosaurs did not suckle their babies on milk, as mammals do.

▶ Various clues from fossil evidence show that the hadrosaur Maiasaura may have brought food back to its newly hatched young in the nest. Whether one parent or both did this is not known.

Some eggs were still not hatched

Preserved eggshells showed signs of trampling by young in the nest

Dinosaur eyes

- **No fossils have been found of dinosaur eyes**, because eyes are soft and squishy, and soon rot away after death, or are eaten by scavengers.

- **The main clues** to dinosaur eyes come from the hollows, or orbits, in the skull where the eyes were located.

- **The orbits** in fossil dinosaur skulls show that dinosaur eyes were similar to those of reptiles today.

- **The 6-m long sauropod** *Vulcanodon* had tiny eyes relative to the size of its head.

- **Small-eyed dinosaurs** probably only had good vision in the daytime.

- **The eyes** of many plant-eating dinosaurs, such

- as *Vulcanodon*, were on the sides of their heads, giving them all-round vision.

- **The small meat-eater** *Troodon* had relatively large eyes, and it could probably see well even in dim light.

- **Troodon's** eyes were on the front of its face and pointed forwards, allowing it to see detail and judge distance.

- **Dinosaurs that had large bulges**, called optic lobes, in their brains – detectable by the shapes of their skulls – could probably see very well, perhaps even at night.

◄ *Leaellynasaura had very large eyes for the size of its skull, suggesting it was active at dusk or at night.*

> ★ STAR FACT ★
> The plant-eater *Leaellynasaura* had large optic lobes, and probably had good eyesight.

Coprolites: Dino-dung

- **Coprolites** are the fossilized droppings, or dung, of animals from long ago, such as dinosaurs.

- **Dinosaur coprolites** are not soft and smelly – like other fossils, they have become solid rock.

- **Many thousands** of dinosaur coprolites have been found at fossil sites all over the world.

- **Cracking or cutting open** coprolites sometimes reveals what the dinosaur had recently eaten.

- **Coprolites** produced by large meat-eaters such as

◄ *Fossilized droppings are no longer squishy or smelly.*

> ★ STAR FACT ★
> One of the largest dinosaur coprolites found measures 44 cm long and was probably produced by *Tyrannosaurus*.

Tyrannosaurus contain bone from their prey.

- **The microscopic structure** of the bones found in coprolites shows the age of the prey when it was eaten. Most victims were very young or old, as these were the easiest creatures for a predator to kill.

- **Coprolites produced by small meat-eaters** such as *Compsognathus* may contain the hard bits of insects, such as the legs and wing-cases of beetles.

- **Huge piles of coprolites** found in Montana, USA, were probably produced by the large plant-eater *Maiasaura*.

- **Maiasaura** coprolites contain the remains of cones, buds and the needlelike leaves of conifer trees, showing that these dinosaurs had a tough diet.

Scelidosaurus

- **Scelidosaurus** was a medium-sized armoured dinosaur, perhaps an early member of the group called the ankylosaurs.

- **Fossils of** Scelidosaurus have been found in North America, Europe and possibly Asia.

- **Scelidosaurus** lived during the Early Jurassic Period, about 200 million years ago.

- **From nose to tail**, Scelidosaurus was about 4 m long.

- **Scelidosaurus** probably moved about on 4 legs, although it could perhaps rear up to gather food.

- **A plant-eater**, Scelidosaurus snipped off its food with the beaklike front of its mouth, and chewed it with its simple, leaf-shaped teeth.

- **Scelidosaurus** is one of the earliest dinosaurs known to have had a set of protective, bony armour plates.

- **A row of about 50 bony plates**, or scutes, stuck up from Scelidosaurus's neck, back and tail.

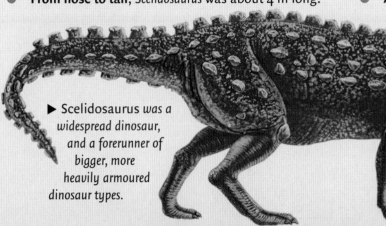

▶ Scelidosaurus *was a widespread dinosaur, and a forerunner of bigger, more heavily armoured dinosaur types.*

- **Scelidosaurus** had rows of conical bony plates along its flanks, resembling limpets on a rock.

- **Scelidosaurus** was described in 1859, and named in 1863, by Richard Owen, who also invented the name 'dinosaur'.

Australia

- **In the past 40 years**, some of the most exciting discoveries of dinosaur fossils have come from Australia.

- **Remains of the large plant-eater** Muttaburrasaurus were found near Muttaburra, Queensland.

- **Muttaburrasaurus** was about 7 m long and similar in some ways to the well-known plant-eater Iguanodon.

- **Fossils of** Rhoetosaurus, a giant plant-eater, were found in 1924 in southern Queensland.

- **The sauropod** Rhoetosaurus was about 17 m long and lived 170 million years ago.

- **Near Winton, Queensland**, more than 3300 footprints

▶ *Many exciting fossils have been found in Australia over the past 40 years - many found nowhere else.*

★ STAR FACT ★
Dinosaur Cove is difficult to reach, and many of the fossils are in hard rocks in the middle of sheer cliffs with pounding waves far beneath.

show where about 130 dinosaurs once passed by.

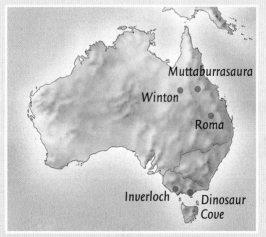

Muttaburrasaura
Winton
Roma
Inverloch
Dinosaur Cove

- **One of the major new fossil sites** in Australia is 'Dinosaur Cove', on the coast near Melbourne, Victoria.

- **Fossil-rich rocks** at 'Dinosaur Cove' are part of the Otway-Strzelecki mountain ranges, and are 120–100 million years old.

- **Remains** found at 'Dinosaur Cove' include Leaellynasaura and a smaller version of the huge meat-eater Allosaurus.

Sauropods

- **The sauropods** were the biggest of all the dinosaurs.

- **The huge plant-eating sauropods** lived mainly during the Jurassic Period, 208–144 million years ago.

- **A typical sauropod** had a tiny head, a very long neck and tail, a huge, bulging body and 4 massive legs, similar to those of an elephant, but much bigger.

- **Sauropods** included the well-known *Mamenchisaurus, Cetiosaurus, Diplodocus, Brachiosaurus* and *Apatosaurus*.

- **Rebbachisaurus** fossils were found in Morocco, Tunisia and Algeria.

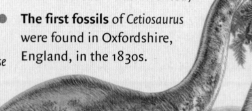

▶ *Sauropods could browse in tree-tops.*

- **Rebbachisaurus** lived 120 million years ago.

- **Cetiosaurus** was about 18 m long and weighed 30 tonnes.

- **Cetiosaurus**, or 'whale reptile', was so-named because French fossil expert Georges Cuvier thought that its giant backbones came from a prehistoric whale.

- **Cetiosaurus** was the first sauropod to be given an official name, in 1841 – the year before the term 'dinosaur' was invented,

- **The first fossils** of *Cetiosaurus* were found in Oxfordshire, England, in the 1830s.

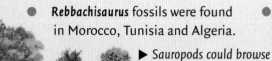

Dinosaur feet

- **Dinosaur feet differed**, depending on the animal's body design, weight and lifestyle.

- **A typical dinosaur's front feet** had metacarpal bones in the lower wrist or upper hand, and 2 or 3 phalanges bones in each digit (finger or toe), tipped by claws.

- **The rear feet** of a typical dinosaur had metatarsal (instead of metacarpal) bones in the lower ankle.

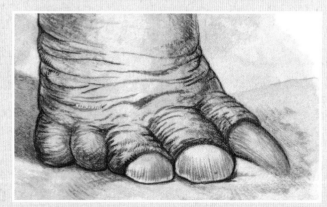

▲ *Each foot of Apatosaurus supported more than 5 tonnes.*

★ STAR FACT ★
The dinosaur group that includes all the meat-eaters, both large and small, is named the theropods, or 'beast feet'.

- **Some dinosaurs had 5 toes** per foot, like most other reptiles (and most birds and mammals).

- **Sauropods** probably had feet with rounded bases supported by a wedge of fibrous, cushion-like tissue.

- **Most sauropods** had claws on their first 3 toes, and smaller, blunter 'hooves' on the other 2 toes.

- **Ostrich-dinosaurs** such as *Gallimimus* had very long feet and long, slim toes for fast running.

- **Many fast-running dinosaurs** had fewer toes, to reduce weight – *Gallimimus* had 3 toes per back foot.

- **The dinosaur group** that includes *Iguanodon*, duck-billed dinosaurs, *Heterodontosaurus* and many other plant-eaters is named the ornithopods, or 'bird feet'.

Extinction

- **All dinosaurs on Earth** had died out, or become extinct, by 65 million years ago.

- **Many other reptiles**, such as pterosaurs and plesiosaurs, and many other animals and plants disappeared with the dinosaurs, in a 'mass extinction'.

- **A possible cause** of the mass extinction was a new kind of disease that swept across the land and seas.

- **The mass extinction** of the dinosaurs and other animals may have been due to a series of huge volcanic eruptions that filled the air with poisonous fumes.

- **Climate change** is another possible cause of the mass extinction – perhaps a period of global warming that lasted for a few hundred years, or even longer.

▼ We can only guess at the havoc caused when a massive meteorite hit Earth 65 million years ago. Whether this was the main cause of the mass extinction, or the 'last straw' following other problems, is not clear from evidence found so far.

> **★ STAR FACT ★**
> Scientists found a huge crater – the Chixulub Crater – under sea-bed mud off the coast of Yucatan, Mexico. This could be where a giant meteorite hit Earth 65 million years ago.

- **One theory** for the mass extinction is that a giant lump of rock from space – a meteorite – hit Earth.

- **A giant meteorite** 10 km across smashing into Earth would have set off earthquakes and volcanoes, and thrown up vast amounts of dust to darken the skies.

- **Skies darkened by dust for 1 year or more** would mean the death of many plants, and so the death of plant-eating animals, and consequently the meat-eaters.

- **One great puzzle** about the disappearance of the dinosaurs is why similar reptiles, such as crocodiles, lizards and turtles, survived.

Dilophosaurus

- **Dilophosaurus** was a large meat-eating dinosaur in the group known as the ceratosaurs.

- **About 200 million years ago**, *Dilophosaurus* roamed the Earth in search of prey.

- **Fossils** of *Dilophosaurus* were found in Arizona, USA, and possibly Yunnan, China.

- **The remains** of *Dilophosaurus* in Arizona, USA, were discovered by Jesse Williams, a Navajo Native American, in 1942.

- **Studying the fossils** of *Dilophosaurus* proved very difficult, and the dinosaur was not given its official name until 1970.

- **Dilophosaurus** measured about 6 m from its nose to the end of its very long tail.

- **The name** *Dilophosaurus* means 'two ridged reptile', from the two thin, rounded, bony crests on its head, each shaped like half a dinner plate.

- **The crests** of *Dilophosaurus* were too thin and fragile to be used as weapons for head-butting.

- **Brightly coloured skin** may have covered *Dilophosaurus's* head crests, as a visual display to rivals or enemies.

> ★ **STAR FACT** ★
> *Dilophosaurus* probably weighed about 500 kg – as much as the biggest polar bears today.

◄ The fearsome *Dilophosaurus* was one of the first large meat-eating dinosaurs. It gained the nickname 'terror of the Early Jurassic'.

Mysteries

- **Some dinosaurs have been named** on very scant evidence, such as a single bit of fossil bone, or just one tooth or claw.

- **The small meat-eater** *Troodon* was named in 1856 on the evidence of a single tooth.

- **The first tooth** of *Troodon* was found in the Judith River region of Montana, USA.

- **At first**, the tooth of *Troodon* was thought to have come from a lizard such as a monitor lizard.

- **In the early 1900s**, more *Troodon*-like teeth were found in Alberta and Wyoming, and were believed to have come from a pachycephalosaur or 'bone-head' dinosaur.

- **In the 1980s**, a fuller picture of *Troodon* was built up by putting its teeth together with other fossils, including bones.

- **Only parts of the hands and arms** of *Deinocheirus* have been found. They were discovered in Mongolia, Central Asia, in the 1970s.

- **It is possible** that *Deinocheirus* was a gigantic ostrich-dinosaur, perhaps as tall as a giraffe, at 5–6 m.

- **Therizinosaurus**, or 'scythe reptile', was a huge dinosaur known only from a few parts of its limbs. It lived in the Late Cretaceous Period in Mongolia, Central Asia.

- **A mysterious fossil claw** was found, thought possibly to belong to *Therizinosaurus*, and measuring about 90 cm around its outer curve.

► Deinocheirus, known only from a few fossil pieces of arm and hand, may have been an ostrich-dinosaur like this – but as tall as a giraffe.

Psittacosaurus

- **Psittacosaurus** was a plant-eater in the group known as the ceratopsians, or horn-faced dinosaurs.

- **Living in the Middle Cretaceous Period**, Psittacosaurus walked the Earth about 115–110 million years ago.

- **Psittacosaurus** was named in 1923 from fossils found in Mongolia, Central Asia.

- **Fossils** of Psittacosaurus have been found at various sites across Asia, including ones in Russia, China and Thailand.

- **The rear legs** of Psittacosaurus were longer and stronger than its front legs, suggesting that this dinosaur may have reared up to run fast on its rear legs, rather than running on all 4 legs.

- **Psittacosaurus** measured about 2 m long.

- **On each foot** Psittacosaurus had 4 toes.

- **The name** Psittacosaurus means 'parrot reptile', after the dinosaur's beak-shaped mouth, like that of a parrot.

- **Inside its cheeks**, Psittacosaurus had many sharp teeth capable of cutting and slicing through tough plant material.

◄ *Psittacosaurus had two small ridges or horns, one on each cheek.*

★ **STAR FACT** ★
Fossil evidence shows that when newly hatched from their eggs, baby Psittacosaurus were hardly longer than a human hand.

Beaks

- **Several kinds of dinosaurs** had a toothless, beak-shaped front to their mouths.

- **Beaked dinosaurs** included ceratopsians (horn-faces) such as *Triceratops*, ornithopods such as *Iguanodon* and the hadrosaurs (duck-bills), stegosaurs, segnosaurs, ankylosaurs (armoured dinosaurs) and fast-running ostrich-dinosaurs.

- **Most beaked dinosaurs** had chopping or chewing teeth near the backs of their mouths, in their cheeks, but ostrich-dinosaurs had no teeth.

- **A dinosaur's beak** was made up of the upper (maxilla) and the lower (mandible) jaw bones.

- **Ornithischian (bird-hipped) dinosaurs** had what is called a 'predentary' bone at the front tip of the lower jaw.

★ **STAR FACT** ★
Some of the largest beaks in relation to body size belonged to *Oviraptor* and Psittacosaurus.

- **Ceratopsian (horn-faced) dinosaurs** had a 'rostral' bone at the front tip of the upper jaw.

- **In life**, the bones at the front of a dinosaur's jaw would have been covered with horn, which formed the outer shape of the beak.

- **Dinosaurs almost certainly** used their beaks for pecking, snipping, tearing and slicing their food.

- **Dinosaurs may have** used their beaks to peck fiercely at any attackers.

◄ *Ornithomimus's long, toothless jaws would have been covered by horny beak.*

Massospondylus

- **Massospondylus** was a medium-sized plant-eater belonging to the group known as the prosauropods.

- **Africa and perhaps North America** were home to *Massospondylus*, about 200 million years ago.

- **In total**, *Massospondylus* was about 5 m long, with almost half of this length being its tail.

- **The rear legs** of *Massospondylus* were bigger and stronger than its front legs, so it may have reared up to reach high-up food.

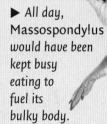

▶ *All day, Massospondylus would have been kept busy eating to fuel its bulky body.*

- **The name** *Massospondylus* means 'huge backbone'.

- **Fossils of more than 80** *Massospondylus* have been found, making it one of the best-studied dinosaurs.

- **Massospondylus** had a tiny head compared to its large body, and it must have spent many hours each day gathering enough food to survive.

- **The front teeth** of *Massospondylus* were surprisingly large and strong for a plant-eater, with ridged edges more like meat-eating teeth.

- **The cheek teeth** of *Massospondylus* were too small and weak for chewing large amounts of plant food, so perhaps the dinosaur's food was mashed mainly in its stomach.

- **In the 1980s**, some scientists suggested that *Massospondylus* may have been a meat-eater, partly because of the ridged edges on its front teeth.

Stomach stones

- **Some dinosaur fossils** are found with unusually smooth, rounded stones, like seashore pebbles, jumbled up among or near them.

- **Smoothed pebbles** occur with dinosaur fossils far more than would be expected by chance alone.

- **Smooth stones** are mainly found with or near the remains of large plant-eating dinosaurs, especially those of prosauropods such as *Massospondylus*, *Plateosaurus* and *Riojasaurus*, sauropods such as *Brachiosaurus* and *Diplodocus*, the parrot-beaked *Psittacosaurus* and the stegosaurs.

- **Some plant-eating dinosaurs** may have used smooth stones to help process their food.

▶ *Gastroliths range from pea- to football-sized.*

- **The smoothed pebbles** associated with dinosaur remains are known as gastroliths, gastric millstones or gizzard stones.

- **Gastroliths** were stones that a dinosaur found on the ground and deliberately swallowed into its stomach.

- **In the dinosaur's stomach**, gastroliths acted as 'millstones', crushing and churning plant food, and breaking it down into a soft pulp for better digestion.

- **As gastroliths churned and rubbed** inside a dinosaur's guts, they became very rounded, smoothed and polished.

- **Gastroliths as small as a pea** and as large as a football have been found.

- **Gastroliths may be the reason why** many big plant-eaters, especially sauropods, had no chewing teeth – the mashing was done inside the guts.

Migration

- **Almost no land reptiles today** go on regular, long-distance journeys, called migrations.

- **Over the past 30 years**, scientists have acquired evidence that some dinosaurs regularly migrated.

- **Evidence for migrating dinosaurs** comes from the positions of the continents at the time. In certain regions, cool winters would have prevented the growth of enough plants for dinosaurs to eat.

- **Fossil evidence suggests** that some plants stopped growing during very hot or dry times, so some

> ★ STAR FACT ★
> Migrating *Centrosaurus* may have walked 100 km a day.

- dinosaurs would have had to migrate to find food.

- **The footprints or tracks** of many dinosaurs travelling in herds is possible evidence that some dinosaurs migrated.

- **Dinosaurs that may have migrated** include *Centrosaurus* and *Pachyrhinosaurus*, sauropods such as *Diplodocus*, and ornithopods such as *Iguanodon* and *Muttaburrasaurus*.

- **One huge fossil site** in Alberta, Canada, contains the fossils of about 1000 *Pachyrhinosaurus* – perhaps a migrating herd that got caught in a flood.

- **In North America**, huge herds of *Centrosaurus* migrated north for the brief sub-Arctic summer, when plants were abundant, providing plentiful food.

- **In autumn**, *Centrosaurus* herds travelled south again to overwinter in the forests.

◀ *Pachyrhinosaurus may have migrated.*

China

- **For centuries**, dinosaur fossils in China were identified as belonging to folklore creatures such as dragons.

- **The first dinosaur fossils** studied scientifically in China were uncovered in the 1930s.

- **Because of China's political isolation in the past**, many dinosaur fossils found there remained unknown to scientists in other countries.

- **From the 1980s**, dinosaur discoveries in almost every province of China have amazed scientists around the globe.

- **A few exciting dinosaur finds** in China have been fakes, such as part of a bird skeleton that was joined to the part-skeleton of a dinosaur along a natural-looking crack in the rock.

- **Some better-known Chinese finds**

> ★ STAR FACT ★
> Of all the world's countries, probably only the USA has more fossil dinosaurs than China.

of dinosaurs include *Mamenchisaurus*, *Psittacosaurus*, *Tuojiangosaurus* and *Avimimus*.

- **Remains** of the prosauropod *Lufengosaurus* were uncovered in China's southern province of Yunnan, in 1941.

- **China's** *Lufengosaurus* lived during the Early Jurassic Period, and measured about 6–7 m long.

- **Many recently found fossils** in China are of feathered dinosaurs.

◀ *Recent fossil finds in China are causing scientists to change many long-held ideas.*

South America

- **Many of the most important discoveries** of dinosaur fossils in the last 30 years were made in South America.

- **Dinosaur fossils have been found** from the north to the south of the continent, in the countries of Colombia, Peru, Chile, Brazil, Uruguay and Argentina.

- **Most dinosaur fossils in South America** have been found on the high grassland, scrub and semi-desert of southern Brazil and Argentina.

- **Some of the earliest known dinosaurs**, such as

Herrerasaurus and *Eoraptor*, lived more than 225 million years ago in Argentina.

- **Some of the last dinosaurs**, such as the sauropods *Saltasaurus* and *Titanosaurus*, lived in Argentina.

- **Fossils of the meat-eating predator** *Piatnitzkyosaurus* come from Cerro Condo in southern Argentina.

- **Piatnitzkyosaurus** was similar to the great predator *Allosaurus* of North America, but at 4–5 m long was less than half its size.

- **Like many dinosaurs in Argentina**, *Piatnitzkyosaurus* lived during the Middle Jurassic Period.

- **Remains of about 10 huge** *Patagosaurus* sauropods were found in the fossil-rich region of Chubut, Argentina, from 1977.

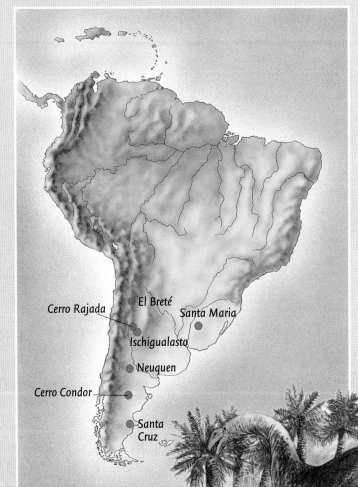

Cerro Rajada

El Breté

Santa Maria

Ischigualasto

Neuquen

Cerro Condor

Santa Cruz

▼ *The high, windswept, stony, grassy plains of southern Argentina are especially rich in Jurassic and Cretaceous fossils, including those of the vast plant-eating sauropods Argentinosaurus. The plains slope upwards to the west, finally reaching the foothills of the Andes, where sun, wind and rain constantly erode the rocks and reveal new remains.*

▲ Dinosaur fossils found in South America since the 1970s reveal unique kinds of meat-eaters, the biggest predatory dinosaurs, some of the earliest members of the dinosaur group, and possibly the largest of all dinosaurs.

Tuojiangosaurus

- **Tuojiangosaurus** was a member of the group called plated dinosaurs, or stegosaurs.

- **The first nearly complete dinosaur skeleton** to be found in China was of a *Tuojiangosaurus*, and excellent fossil skeletons are on display in several Chinese museums.

- **The name** *Tuojiangosaurus* means 'Tuo River reptile'.

- **Tuojiangosaurus** lived during the Late Jurassic Period, about 155 million years ago.

- **Tuojiangosaurus** was 7 m long from nose to tail-tip.

- **The weight of** *Tuojiangosaurus* was probably about 1 tonne.

- **Like other stegosaurs**, *Tuojiangosaurus* had tall slabs or plates of bone on its back.

- **The back plates of** *Tuojiangosaurus* were roughly triangular and probably stood upright in 2 rows that ran from the neck to the middle of the tail.

- **Tuojiangosaurus** plucked low-growing plant food with the beak-shaped front of its mouth, and partly chewed the plant material with its leaf-shaped, ridge-edged cheek teeth.

- **On its tail**, *Tuojiangosaurus* had 4 long spikes arranged in two Vs, which it could swing at enemies to keep them at a distance or inflict wounds.

◀ Tuojiangosaurus had about 15 pairs of tall plates along its neck, back and tail.

Head crests

- **Many dinosaurs** had lumps, bumps, plates, bulges, ridges or other shapes of bone on their heads, called head crests.

- **Head crests** may have been covered with brightly coloured skin in life, for visual display.

- **Meat-eaters with head crests** included *Carnotaurus* and *Dilophosaurus*.

- **The dinosaurs with the largest** and most complicated head crests were the hadrosaurs.

- **The largest dinosaur head crest** was probably a long, hollow, tubular shape of bone belonging to the hadrosaur *Parasaurolophus*.

- **The head crests of hadrosaurs** may have been involved in making sounds.

- **Some years ago** the hadrosaur *Tsintaosaurus* was thought to have a very unusual head crest – a hollow tube sticking straight up between the eyes, like a unicorn's horn.

- **The so-called head crest** of *Tsintaosaurus* is now thought to be the fossil part of another animal, and not part of *Tsintaosaurus* at all.

- **Tsintaosaurus** is now usually known as *Tanius*, a hadrosaur with a small crest or no crest at all!

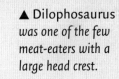

▲ Dilophosaurus was one of the few meat-eaters with a large head crest.

> ★ STAR FACT ★
> The head crests of some large
> *Parasaurolophus*, perhaps full-grown males,
> reached an incredible 1.8 m in length.

Sails

- **Long, bony extensions**, like rods or spines, stuck up from the backs of some dinosaurs.

- **In life**, a dinosaur's bony extensions may have held up a large area of skin, commonly called a back sail.

- **Dinosaurs with back sails** included the huge meat-eater *Spinosaurus* and the large plant-eater *Ouranosaurus*.

- **Spinosaurus** and *Ouranosaurus* both lived over 100 million years ago.

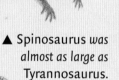

▲ *Spinosaurus was almost as large as Tyrannosaurus.*

- **Fossils of** *Spinosaurus* and *Ouranosaurus* were found in North Africa.

- **The skin** on a dinosaur's back sail may have been brightly coloured, or may even have changed colour, like the skin of a chameleon lizard today.

▲ *Apart from its sail, Ouranosaurus was similar to its close cousin, the plant-eater Iguanodon.*

- **A dinosaur's back sail** may have helped to control its body temperature.

- **Standing sideways** to the sun, a back sail would absorb the sun's heat and allow the dinosaur to warm up quickly, ready for action.

- **Standing in the shade**, a back sail would lose warmth and help the dinosaur to avoid overheating.

- **The bony back rods** of *Spinosaurus* were up to 1.6 m tall.

North America

- **North America** is the continent where most dinosaur fossils have been found.

- **Most dinosaur fossils** in North America come from the dry, rocky 'badlands' of the Midwest region, which includes Alberta in Canada, and the US states of Montana, Wyoming, Utah, Colorado and Arizona.

- **Fossils of the most famous dinosaurs** come from North America, including *Allosaurus*, *Tyrannosaurus*, *Diplodocus*, *Triceratops* and *Stegosaurus*.

- **Several fossil-rich sites** in North America are now national parks.

- **The US Dinosaur National Monument**, on the border of Utah and Colorado, was established in 1915.

- **The Cleveland-Lloyd Dinosaur Quarry** in Utah contains fossils of stegosaurs, ankylosaurs, sauropods and meat-eaters such as *Allosaurus*.

- **Along the Red Deer River** in Alberta, a large area with thousands of dinosaur fossils has been designated the Dinosaur Provincial Park.

- **Fossils found in Alberta** include those of the meat-eater *Albertosaurus*, armoured *Euoplocephalus* and the duck-bill *Lambeosaurus*.

- **The Dinosaur Provincial Park** in Alberta is a United Nations World Heritage Site – the same status as the pyramids of ancient Egypt.

- **A huge, 20-m long plant-eater** was named *Alamosaurus* after the famous Battle of the Alamo in Texas in 1836.

▲ *Some of the most famous dinosaurs lived in the areas marked above.*

Iguanodon

- **Iguanodon** was a large plant-eater in the dinosaur group known as ornithopods.

- **Numerous fossils** of *Iguanodon* have been found in several countries in Europe, including England, Belgium, Germany and Spain.

- **Iguanodon** measured about 9 m from nose to tail.

- **It is estimated** that an *Iguanodon* weighed about the same as a large elephant - 4–5 tonnes.

- **Iguanodon** lived during the Early to Middle Cretaceous Period, 140–110 million years ago.

- **Iguanodon** probably walked and ran on its large, powerful back legs for much of the time, with its body held horizontal.

- **A cone-shaped spike** on *Iguanodon's* thumb may have been a weapon for jabbing at rivals or enemies.

★ STAR FACT ★

Iguanodon was one of the very first dinosaurs to be given an official scientific name, in 1825.

- **The 3 central fingers** on *Iguanodon's* hands had hooflike claws for occasional four-legged walking.

- **The fifth or little finger** of *Iguanodon* was able to bend across the hand for grasping objects, and was perhaps used to pull plants towards the mouth.

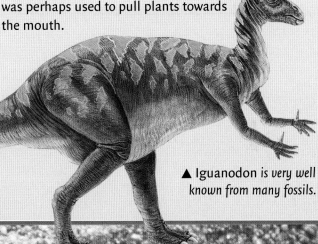

▲ Iguanodon *is very well known from many fossils.*

Hibernation

- **Dinosaurs may have gone into an inactive state** called hibernation during long periods of cold conditions, as many reptiles do today.

- **Dinosaurs** such as the small plant-eater *Leaellynasaura*, found at 'Dinosaur Cove', Australia, may have had to hibernate due to the yearly cycle of seasons there.

- **Dinosaur Cove, Australia**, was nearer the South Pole when dinosaurs lived there, 120–100 million years ago.

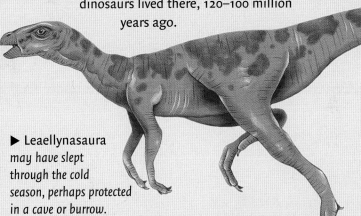

▶ Leaellynasaura *may have slept through the cold season, perhaps protected in a cave or burrow.*

- **The climate** was relatively warm 120–100 million years ago, with no ice at the North or South Poles.

- **Dinosaurs at Dinosaur Cove, Australia**, would have had to cope with long hours of darkness during winter, when few plants grew.

- **Australia's Dinosaur Cove dinosaurs** may have hibernated for a few months each year to survive the cool, dark conditions.

- **The eyes and brain shape** of *Leaellynasaura* from Dinosaur Cove, Australia, suggest that this dinosaur had good eyesight.

- *Leaellynasaura* may have needed good eyesight to see in the winter darkness, or in the dim forests.

- **Dinosaur fossils** have been found in the Arctic region near the North Pole.

- **Arctic dinosaurs** either hibernated during winter, or migrated south to warmer regions.

Sounds

- **Few reptiles today make sounds**, except for simple hisses, grunts and coughs.

- **Fossils suggest that dinosaurs** made a variety of sounds in several different ways.

- **The bony, hollow head crests** of duck-bills (hadrosaurs) may have been used for making sounds.

- **The head crests of some hadrosaurs** contained tubes called respiratory airways, used for breathing.

- **Air** blown forcefully through a hadrosaur's head crest passages could have made the whole crest vibrate.

- **A hadrosaur's vibrating head crest** may have made a loud sound like a honk, roar or bellow – similar to an elephant trumpeting with its trunk.

- **Fossil skulls** of some hadrosaurs, such as *Edmontosaurus* and *Kritosaurus*, suggest

that there was a loose flap of skin, like a floppy bag, between the nostrils and the eyes.

- *Kritosaurus* may have inflated its loose nasal flap of skin like a balloon to make a honking or bellowing sound, as some seals do today.

- **Dinosaurs may have made sounds** to keep in touch with other members of their herd, to frighten away enemies, to intimidate rivals and to impress potential mates at breeding time.

◀ In a battle between predator and prey, Tyrannosaurus may have been startled or even warned off by the trumpeting of Parasaurolophus. The effect of the sudden noise on the predator may have given the plant-eating hadrosaur time to escape. Its noise may also have summoned members of its herd, for massed defence against the huge meat-eater.

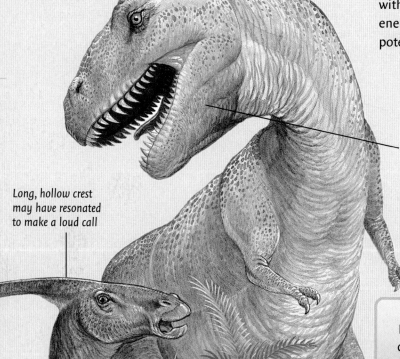

Long, hollow crest may have resonated to make a loud call

Tyrannosaurus may have been startled by the noise of its prey

★ STAR FACT ★

By blowing through models of hadrosaur head crests, a wide range of sounds can be made – a bit like those of brass and wind instruments!

Powerful rear legs used for kicking in self defence

Tail used for lashing out

Nodosaurs

- **Nodosaurs** were a subgroup of armoured dinosaurs, in the main ankylosaur group.

- **The nodosaur subgroup** included *Edmontonia*, *Sauropelta*, *Polacanthus* and *Nodosaurus*.

- **Nodosaurs were slow-moving**, heavy-bodied plant-eaters with thick, heavy nodules, lumps and plates of bone in their skin for protection.

- **Most nodosaurs lived** during the Late Jurassic and the Cretaceous Periods, 150–65 million years ago.

- **Edmontonia** lived in North America during the Late Cretaceous Period, 75–70 million years ago.

- **Edmontonia** was about 7 m long, but its bony armour made it very heavy for its size, at 4–5 tonnes.

★ STAR FACT ★
Like many nodosaurs, *Edmontonia* and *Polacanthus* probably had long, fierce spikes on their shoulders, used to 'spear' enemies.

- **Along its neck, back and tail** *Edmontonia* had rows of flat and spiky plates.

- **The nodosaur** *Polacanthus* was about 4 m long and lived 120–110 million years ago.

- **Fossils** of *Polacanthus* come from the Isle of Wight, southern England, and perhaps from North America, in South Dakota, USA.

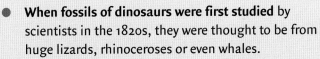

◀ *Edmontonia, one of the last dinosaurs, was covered in many sharp lumps of bone that gave it some protection from its enemies.*

Inventing the 'dinosaur'

- **When fossils of dinosaurs were first studied** by scientists in the 1820s, they were thought to be from huge lizards, rhinoceroses or even whales.

- **The first dinosaur** to be given an official name was *Megalosaurus*, by English clergyman William Buckland in 1824.

- **Fossils of dinosaurs** were found and studied in 1822 by Gideon Mantell, a country doctor in Sussex, southern England.

- **In 1825**, Englishman Gideon Mantell named his creature *Iguanodon*, because its fossil teeth were very similar in shape to, but larger than, the teeth of the iguana lizard.

- **In the late 1830s**, British scientist Richard Owen realized that some fossils did not belong to lizards, but to an as yet unnamed group of reptiles.

- **In 1841–42**, Richard Owen invented a new name for the group of giant prehistoric reptiles – Dinosauria.

- **The name 'dinosaur'** means 'terrible reptile'.

- **Life-sized models** of several dinosaurs were made by sculptor Waterhouse Hawkins in 1852–54.

- **Hawkins' models** were displayed in the gardens of the Crystal Palace Exhibition in London, and caused a public sensation – the first wave of 'Dino-mania'.

- **The three main dinosaurs** of the Dinosauria in the 1840s were *Iguanodon*, the big meat-eater *Megalosaurus* and the nodosaur *Hyaelosaurus*.

◀ *Megalosaurus was the first dinosaur to be given an official scientific name, even though the term 'dinosaur' had not yet been invented.*

Brains

- **There is a broad link** between the size of an animal's brain compared to the size of its body, and the level of intelligence it shows.

- **Some fossil dinosaur skulls** have preserved the hollow where the brain once was, revealing the approximate size and shape of the brain.

- **In some cases** a lump of rock formed inside a fossil skull, taking on the size and shape of the brain.

- **The tiny brain** of *Stegosaurus* weighed about 70–80 g, while the whole dinosaur weighed up to 2 tonnes.

- **The brain** of *Stegosaurus* was only 1/25,000th of the weight of its whole body (in a human it is 1/50th).

- **Brachiosaurus's** brain was perhaps only 1/100,000th of the weight of its whole body.

- **The brain of the small meat-eater** *Troodon* was about 1/100th the weight of its whole body.

▶ *Troodon may have been fairly 'intelligent' for a dinosaur.*

- **The brain-body size comparison** for most dinosaurs is much the same as the brain-body size for living reptiles.

- **Small and medium sized meat-eaters** such as *Troodon* may have been as 'intelligent' as parrots or rats.

- **It was once thought** that *Stegosaurus* had a 'second brain' in the base of its tail! Now this lump is thought to have been a nerve junction.

Segnosaurs

- **Little is known** about the segnosaur group of dinosaurs – the subject of much disagreement among experts.

- **Segnosaurs** are named after almost the only known member of the group, *Segnosaurus*.

- **The name** *Segnosaurus* means 'slow reptile'.

- *Segnosaurus* lived during the Mid to Late Cretaceous Period, about 90 million years ago.

- **Fossils** of *Segnosaurus* were found mainly in the Gobi Desert in

Central Asia in the 1970s. The dinosaur was named in 1979 by Mongolian scientist Altangerel Perle.

- *Segnosaurus* had a narrow head and probably a toothless, beaklike front to its mouth.

- **Experts have variously described** *Segnosaurus* as a predatory meat-eater, a swimming or wading fish-eater, a rearing-up leaf-eater, or even an ant-eater.

- **Different experts have said** *Segnosaurus* was a theropod, a prosauropod and an ornithopod.

- **Some scientists have suggested** that *Segnosaurus* was a huge dinosaur-version of today's anteater that ripped open the nests of termites and ants with its powerful claws.

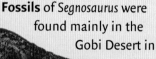

▶ *Segnosaurus remains a mystery – even its diet is hotly debated by the experts.*

★ STAR FACT ★
Segnosaurus was a sizeable dinosaur, probably about 6 m long and standing 2 m tall.

Dino-birds: 2

- **Fossils found during the last 20 years** show that some dinosaurs may have been covered with feathers or fur.

- *Sinosauropteryx* was a small, 1-m long meat-eater that lived 135 million years ago in China.

- **Fossils** of *Sinosauropteryx* show that parts of its body were covered not with the usual reptile scales, but with feathers.

- **The overall shape** of *Sinosauropteryx* shows that, despite being feathered, it could not fly.

- **The feathers** of *Sinosauropteryx* may have been for camouflage, for visual display, or to keep it warm – suggesting it was warm-blooded.

- *Avimimus* was a small, light dinosaur. Its fossils come from China and Mongolia, and date from 85–82 million years ago.

- **The 1.5-m long** *Avimimus* had a mouth shaped like a bird's beak for pecking at food.

- **The fossil arm bones** of *Avimimus* have small ridges of the same size and shape as the ridges on birds' wing bones, where feathers attach.

- **In modern science**, any animal with feathers is a bird, so some experts say that feathered dinosaurs were not actually dinosaurs or even reptiles, but birds.

- **Some experts say** that birds are not really a separate group of animals, but a subgroup of dinosaurs that lives on today, and they should be regarded as feathered dinosaurs.

▲ *Avimimus may have evolved feathers for warmth or for camouflage.*

After dinosaurs

- **The Age of Dinosaurs** came to a fairly sudden end 65 million years ago. We know this from rocks and fossils, which changed dramatically at that time.

- **The Cretaceous Period** ended 65 million years ago.

- **There are no dinosaur fossils** since 65 million years ago.

- **Many animal groups**, including fish, crocodiles, turtles, lizards, birds and mammals, survived the extinction that took place 65 million years ago.

- **Birds and mammals** in particular underwent rapid changes after the dinosaurs disappeared.

- **Within 10 million years** of the dinosaurs' demise, bats, primates, armadillos, hoofed mammals and rodents such as rats had all appeared.

- **The land mammal** that came closest to rivalling the great size of the dinosaurs was *Indricotherium*, also known as *Baluchitherium*.

- *Indricotherium* was 8 m long, 5 m tall and weighed perhaps 25 tonnes.

- *Indricotherium* was less than half the size of the biggest dinosaurs.

▶ *Indricotherium was 3 times bigger than elephants of today.*

★ **STAR FACT** ★
Some people believe that dinosaurs may still be alive today, deep in tropical forests or in remote valleys – but no firm evidence exists.

INDEX

Acknowledgements

Artists: Chris Buzer (Galante Studio), Jim Channell, Brian Delf, Fiametta Dogi (Scientific Illustrations), Chris Forsey, L R Galante (Galante Studio),Shami Ghale, Alan Hancocks, Steve Kirk, Kevin Maddison, Alan Male (Linden Artists), Janos Marffy, Gill Platt, Terry Riley, Steve Roberts, Guy Smith (Mainline Design), Sarah Smith, Rudi Vizi, Christian Webb (Temple Rogers), Steve Weston, Mike White (Temple Rogers)

The publisher would like to thank the following source for the use of their photograph: p43 Kobal Collection/Amblin/Universal

All other photographs are from: MKP Archives; Corbis Professional Collections; Corel Corporation; PhotoDisk